re-think

To Paige -
very best wishes
Nigel

We have worked with Nigel and his technique for many years, and re-thinking has proven to be a source of 'new thinking', not just once, but continuously. It has been inspirational as well as practical, which has enabled us to continue to go from strength to strength and stay a leader in our field.

Karin Forseke, CEO
Carnegie Investment Bank AB

Our senior Occupational Health team have been working with these ideas and the result has been the development for the first time of a clear definition of what world-class excellence means in our profession, and how this can be translated from grandiose words into measurable actions and benefits. We could not have achieved this without the extra creativity from Nigel as a catalyst.

Dr John Cooper, Head of Corporate Occupational Health
Unilever

re-think

how to think differently

Nigel May Barlow

First published 2006 by
Capstone Publishing Limited (a Wiley Company)
The Atrium
Southern Gate
Chichester
West Sussex
PO19 8SQ
www.wileyeurope.com
Email (for orders and customer service enquires): cs-books@wiley.co.uk

British Library Cataloguing in Publication Data
A catalogue record for this book is available from the British Library

ISBN-13: 978-1-84112-695-1 (PB)

Typeset in Adobe Garamond by Sparks – www.sparks.co.uk
Printed and bound in Great Britain by TJ International Ltd, Padstow, Cornwall

This book is printed on acid-free paper responsibly manufactured from sustainable forestry in which at least two trees are planted for each one used for paper production.
Substantial discounts on bulk quantities of Capstone Books are available to corporations, professional associations and other organizations.
For details telephone John Wiley & Sons on (+44) 1243-770441, fax (+44) 1243 770571 or email corporatedevelopment@wiley.co.uk
10 9 8 7 6 5 4 3

RE-THINK

noun, verb

1 To discover different, better, or new ways of approaching familiar problems and situations.

2 To develop ways of achieving this.

3 To have the courage to put new ideas into practice.

4 An insight that's a fresh take.

YES, BUT

noun, verb

1 To evaluate and judge an idea even before you've fully heard it.

2 An attitude that's adverse to fresh thinking.

3 Having the mindset of a critic rather than a creator.

Barlow's Creative Dictionary, Oxford, 2006

contents

Thank you ix
Dedication x
Introduction 1

1 **The way we see things** **11**
Borrowing the perceptions of others 23
New fantasies, new heroes 28
Spring-clean your beliefs 33

2 **Awakening curiosity** **39**
Open-page thinking 53
New people, new ideas 57
Things to be curious about 62

3 **Intuition and eureka** **71**
Accelerating eurekas 84
Mind the gap 88
Idleness and the environment for intuition 92

4 **Paying attention** **99**
Taking a bat's view 116
Family rituals 120
There's no present like the time 125

5	**Co-creation**	**131**
	Blue thinking	144
	A question of style	148
6	**Funny bones**	**151**
	Ah-aha-haha!	161
7	**Simply beautiful**	**171**
	Surround yourself with beauty	183
8	**Storytime!**	**187**
	Writing and living your story	200
9	**Meditation**	**211**
	Just do it!	224
10	**You, me, us – relationships**	**225**
	Relate!	243
11	**The biggest re-think of all**	**247**
	Coda – Acting as if	**255**
	Appendix 1 – The *Re-Think* research	**257**
	Appendix 2 – *Re-think* resources	**271**
About Nigel Barlow		275
Index		277

Thank you

A big thank you to all of the individuals and companies I have worked with on re-thinking over the years. Particularly for putting some very challenging projects my way.

Especially I would like to thank: Charles Cunningham for his scientific clarity; Angie Kaye for her support and re-thinks; my friends and colleagues Ian Taylor and Robert Maguire; Michael Rant for re-think examples; Paul Gerhardt for friendship and ideas; Dr Stephen Steinhaus for designing the survey that influenced this book; my insightful agent Caroline Davidson, and John Moseley at Capstone who has been a highly perceptive and supportive champion of this book. And to those of you around the world who filled in the survey! Also Richard Thompson and all my re-think heroes for creative inspiration.

If I've left anyone off this list, it's down to pure malice rather than a faulty memory.

Most of all to Janet Hanson, who helped to create the book and without whom it simply wouldn't have been possible.

Re-Think is dedicated to

My mother Jean

My family – Angie, Jamie, and Rosie

and

The memory of

my cousin Janice

Introduction

Re-Think will open your mind to fresh possibilities in your everyday life and help you to recapture a childlike sense of curiosity. To re-think means to see different and better solutions to any problem, whether you want to reorganize your life, become closer to your partner, or create a new business idea. All that's needed is for you to put the power of your attention on creative re-thinking and you can't help but have better ideas.

We should all be re-thinkers. Here's why.

A re-thinker has:

- openness to different and better solutions;
- techniques to see the familiar in a fresh light;
- a default setting that thinks 'why not?' 'what if?' rather than 'yes, but';
- ways of accessing deeper levels of thought;

- knowledge of how to create more eureka moments; and
- the courage and will to put new ideas into practice.

A re-thinker is a dreamer who does!

Of course, thinking differently doesn't always produce a better or more useful solution. I live in Oxford, a city of thinkers. During the Second World War a philosopher don from one of the colleges convinced the government that he couldn't be called up for military service because he was, in fact, a duck. He used the full weight of his formidable intelligence to construct an invincible argument on this point. Presumably the intellectual resources of the nation were deployed on more vital issues than out-philosophizing this man.

This is an instance of being able to think differently without thinking better, especially as his cleverness rebounded on him. When he applied for a driving licence after the war, even a bureaucrat could point out the simple truth that ducks don't drive. To re-think means not just to think differently for the sake of it – stimulating though that can be – but to also come up with better solutions.

I've spent much of the last 25 years helping people – individuals, teams and organizations – to see their situation in fresh and creative ways: their lives, careers, personal development, relationships, and businesses. This has taken me to six continents, working with groups as varied as Korean engineers, BBC programme makers, Swedish bankers, and American beer retailers.

I have to tell you it's not all been a picnic: there are some very fixed mindsets out there. And that's just the experts on creativity. Many of them have been using the same examples for the last 25 years. Which is why I prefer the word re-think to creativity.

Re-thinking does encompass the idea of creativity, and at times I will interchange the concepts. But unfortunately words have limiting associations. Creativity is too often stereotyped as something that happens in the arts, in research science, the minds of inventors, in the media, or perhaps in advertising where people are even given the label 'creatives'.

I want to engage you in thinking of creativity in a way that seeps into and infuses every area of your life, not just an approach you roll out for a formal brainstorming session. Inventor Buckminster Fuller decided he wanted to make his life like a trim tab for the planet. A trim tab is a small part of a boat's rudder, which despite its insignificant size has the power to gradually turn the direction of the whole vessel. *Re-think* is like a trim tab that can help you guide your life in different and better directions.

THINKING AS UNUSUAL: EIGHT GREAT RE-THINKS

To get us started here's a list of re-thinks to show what breakthroughs can result from thinking differently and challenging received wisdom in a variety of fields. Thinking as *un*usual. It's *not* intended as a Top 8: I'll leave that to the TV programme makers who seem increasingly unable to think in any way but lists! (Presenting *connections* between different musicians, artists, and performers would be a far more interesting approach.)

You can take any of the principles of re-thinking from these examples and start applying them to a problem right now. They are all ways of thinking afresh, of coming up with new or just better solutions. Re-thinks.

1 Reversing the obvious 1: The Fosbury Flop

Dick Fosbury is an American athlete who revolutionized the high jump by leaping backwards over the bar. In the 1968 Olympics in Mexico City he won the Gold medal and set a new Olympic record. Now almost all modern high jumpers use Fosbury's backwards 'flop'.

Re-think: Turn the problem you're facing on its head; approach it backwards.

2 Taking a big risk: The South African Truth And Reconciliation Commission (TRC)

After the end of apartheid the TRC enabled anyone who had been a victim of violence to come forward and give testimony, much of which was televised nationally and internationally. No one was exempt – this included members of the African National Congress as well as the South African police. Perpetrators of crimes could also give testimony and request amnesty. Though not perfect, it's generally regarded as a great success and a refreshing re-think on 'an eye for an eye and a tooth for a tooth'.

Re-think: Who do you need to get together with to clear the past?

3 Pushing beyond the limits: *Like A Rolling Stone* by Bob Dylan

This 1965 release – rated in *Rolling Stone* magazine as the greatest popular song of all time – was not only semi-improvised, but also challenged the artistic and business conventions of its time by running to six minutes in length. The prevailing mindset was that you couldn't have a song more than three minutes long because people just wouldn't listen to it all the way through. Columbia came up with their own solution to the problem by putting half of the song on each side of the record.

Re-think: What are the self-limiting boundaries you need to break to come up with new solutions?

4 Thinking both/and: Most products from Apple

Combining technology with design, beauty with functionality, is one of the great contributions of Apple. Founder Steven Jobs is passionate about putting together musicians, artists, and even historians with the nerds. The difference shows in a world of grey boxes. The iPod is the first piece of technology that I think is beautiful.

Re-think: How can you combine seemingly unrelated fields and people to produce more beautiful solutions?

5 Reversing the obvious 2: Copernicus' discovery of heliocentricity

Nicolaus Copernicus developed the sun-centred theory of the solar system at the beginning of the sixteenth century in a way that was detailed enough to make it scientifically valuable. Interestingly, astronomy was just a hobby of his, and yet his findings that the earth was not in fact at the centre of the solar system opened the floodgates for the modern scientific revolution, and was a profound challenge to religious views of a geocentric universe.

Re-think: Consider what are the most fundamental assumptions you're making about a situation and challenge them one by one.

6 Re-writing the rulebook: Wikipedia online encyclopedia

Wikipedia is an encyclopedia written by its users, which anyone can add an entry to – and it's free. Founder Jimmy Wales has a mission to make much of human knowledge free and in the public domain. If you're worried about accuracy, a scientist deliberately introduced 13 errors to the encyclopedia, most of which were corrected by subscribers within hours. The world's first encyclopedia was launched in 1743; the impact of Wikipedia may be just as great.

Re-think: How can you use enthusiasts to rewrite the rulebook in your own field?

7 Beautifying the bland: Artwork on garage doors

A service yard door in a Basingstoke, UK, shopping centre has been made a work of art by silversmith Chris Knight, and nominated for a prestigious prize. Knight has become an evangelist for bringing more style to everyday and overlooked industrial objects. The way the light shines through the garage doors is reminiscent of Moorish art. He has also brought beauty to metalwork in a Gateshead multi-storey car park in the northeast of England.

Re-think: Don't assume anything has to be what its stereotype suggests.

8 Selling a story: The Body Shop

The success and the reputation of Body Shop are not based on the products (e.g. Peppermint Foot Lotion) that it sells. Instead, customers feel they are buying into the values of charismatic founder Anita Roddick. Her campaigning against animal testing and ecological plundering is a big part of why many customers buy her products. Increasingly, the story behind what you do is becoming as important as the product or service itself.

Re-think: What's your story?

These examples should give you the idea that there is nothing too big or too small to re-think, and no limit to the strategies you use. You can apply a re-think to anything.

Of course, the assumption behind re-thinking is that we *have* thought in the first place. Once I was coaching a16-year-old girl in study skills. She put down her book, fixed me with a keen gaze and said, 'It's hard to *re*vise something, when you haven't *vised* it in the first place.'

The poet Robert Frost observed that 'the human brain is a wonderful thing. It starts functioning as soon as we wake in the morning – and stops the minute we enter the office.' Unfortunately there is much truth in this. It's possible to stay on automatic pilot and sleepwalk through life without really paying attention to the infinite possibilities that exist all around us.

Re-Think aims to make you more aware of your own thinking process, helping you to switch into another creative gear when you need it.

RE-THINK RESEARCH

Many of the examples in the book come from my experience of helping individuals and companies to creatively re-think. There's also much from my obsessive reading about music, art, business, and the role that creativity plays in diverse fields. Also, from what I prefer to call 'pro-search' – exploring the imaginations of others about the future.

More analytically, I used a survey that over 100 people from around the world responded to. This uncovered some fascinating information on how people think about their own creativity, the role it plays in their lives, and the conditions needed to trigger it. A detailed summary of the survey is in the Appendix, where you might be intrigued to find out which people are most commonly thought of as creative.

What's interesting is how similar are many people's descriptions of creativity, even though couched in different language. A significant finding of the research is that while most see creativity as key to their success and happiness in life, very few have ever received any coaching in it. This is why *Re-Think* was written.

NAVIGATING THE BOOK

It would be great if colleges had to offer courses that combined a practical skill with book learning: Latin and metalwork, carpentry and theology, psychology and plastering might be a good start.

Similarly, *Re-Think* is about philosophy and plumbing – in other words, theory and practice. The first part of each chapter is philosophy/theory, followed by a number of re-thinks; more practical avenues for using the ideas.

There are practical re-thinks throughout the book, which are indicated by the symbol in the margin. It will usually be an action – such as 'buy a new newspaper' – and sometimes a fresh idea to reflect upon.

If you're standing in a bookshop skimming through *Re-Think*, you could read the whole of it by following these symbols in the text. However, sometimes understanding the why behind the idea can change your mind as much as the action. To get you used to this practical way of reading *Re-Think*, here's an example to start with.

Using words without thought can be a barrier to thinking differently. One of the ways in which you can get a shot of re-thinking in the shortest time available is to have a dictionary of word origins in your bathroom. Not only will this impress visitors, but you'll often find a prompt that will open fresh ways of thinking.

Take a word like 'disease' for instance. More usefully, we can think of it as dis-ease. But what if we were to take this insight further? Given that stress creates or aggravates 80 per cent of all illnesses, don't we need a Minister For Ease? And why shouldn't he or she be responsible for reducing stress and increasing ease in all areas of life: health, education, even transport, and dealing with social services?

So buy this dictionary, find a word that's relevant to a project you're working on at home or in the office, discover its origins and, as in the example above, explore its implications.

The way to read this book is to have a specific problem or situation in your mind before you start a chapter; I'd advise one big one and one small one. Your mind will be more committed to resolving the issue if you write it down or even draw it before you start reading.

Don't navigate your way through the book passively. I encourage you to put it down – frequently – and consider, act upon, or discuss the ideas it introduces. There aren't many checklists in *Re-Think* because I'm not sure that they work. Mark the book, tear pages out, make it your own. You might find it useful to have a stack of Post-it Notes and a journal to sketch, and note the ideas that come to you while reading.

Re-Think encourages you to *experience* different ways of thinking, behaving, and being. It's a provocation, a series of insights, and a journey to inspire your creativity. I've intended the first four chapters to be the cornerstones and believe there is some value in reading them in order. But if I were you, I'd dip in anywhere that looks interesting, provided you agree to following the advice about writing down what it is you want to re-think before reading.

Re-thinking doesn't just come from intellectual analysis. Often a poem can set us thinking …

Things To Think

Think in ways you've never thought before.
If the phone rings, think of it as carrying a message
Larger than anything you've ever heard,
Vaster than a hundred lines of Yeats.
Think that someone may bring a bear to your door,
Maybe wounded and deranged; or think that a moose
Has risen out of the lake, and he's carrying on his antlers
A child of your own whom you've never seen.
When someone knocks on the door, think that he's about
To give you something large: tell you you're forgiven,
Or that it's not necessary to work all the time, or that it's
Been decided that if you lie down no one will die.

Robert Bly[1]

Should you re-think everything? No – you'd go crazy. I believe there is a joy in continuity, in keeping some things the same, and preserving what's good. But when you need to be a re-thinker, here's how.

---

1 'Things to Think' from *Morning Poems*, Robert Bly, HarperPerennial, 1997, p. 12. Copyright © 1997 by Robert Bly. Reprinted by permission of HarperCollins Publishers.

re-think one

The way we see things

Our human blind spot is not the physical one at the point where nerves leave the retina of the eye, but our unconscious assumption that the world is as we see it. The one thing I cannot share with you, even if we are in love, is to perceive the world the way you do.

I'd like to draw you in to different ways of *experiencing* how our minds create the world we know. I have an unusual way of introducing myself at conferences. Instead of telling people about myself, about 15 minutes into a presentation I ask people to introduce *me* by responding to questions about my age, background, family, and so on.

Try it for yourself. Here's my photograph. Write down the answers in the spaces below:

Age ......

Education (if any) ....

Last real job (if any) ....

Marital status/kids ....

Car I drive ....

My dream car ....

Newspaper I read ....

Hobbies/interests ....

When I'm with an audience it's amazing what they can write about me in a couple of minutes. How do these impressions register so quickly? People readily answer that it's based on perception, experience, mannerisms, tone of voice, and a score of other tiny indicators. They are right in all this, but of course it doesn't stop them from getting most of the answers wrong.

You haven't had some of these cues, but it's unlikely to have stopped you making what you think are fairly accurate guesses!

My beard has a strong influence on people's answers. Although this is relatively recent in my life, it creates the perception that I studied psychology, sociology or something arty, drive a Volvo or Saab, am a member of Greenpeace, interested in saving the Welsh whale, knit my own yoghurt, and read a left-wing newspaper like the *Guardian*. In fact, most of this is incorrect, but it's extraordinary how immediate one small visual cue is in creating a whole, rich world of associations.

Of course, the answers don't matter. If you feel a bit cheated and are seriously interested, do email me. The point is that we are all making up a story of reality in our minds, which we rarely stop to reflect upon, and often unconsciously impose on others. For instance, I remember giving the task above to a Spanish group who said that I drove a Ford Mondeo.

'No, I don't.'

'Well, you *should*.'

They then took me on a test drive in one of their Mondeos at lunch-time!

The serious danger here is that you and I both stereotype people and problems – often based on limited or superficial information – and all of us have been stereotyped at some time in our life or career. So when somebody says, 'My first impressions are never mistaken', this is a self-fulfilling prophecy because it's rarely checked.

The amazing thing is how little conscious data we need to make up an inner story about other people and situations. Whenever you or I are a customer, we only need one experience with the restaurant, hotel, or shop before we have made up our minds to love or hate it. When people say to me that they needed *no* data to tell me a lot about myself, I don't think they are saying they are telepathic, but rather that we are not conscious of the thousands of bits of data our brains sift every second before producing a stereotyped, familiar picture of the world.

The conclusion is startling: most of the time you and I are not thinking – we are merely stereotyping. Think about it.

How perception happens

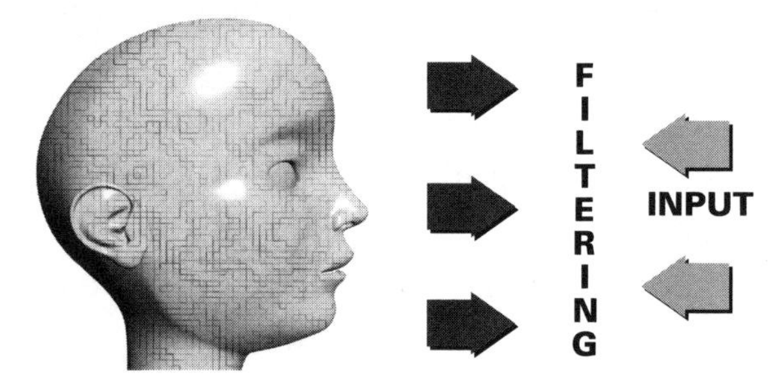

The picture of the perceptual grid above is a highly simplified rendition of how we see the world. We receive input from the outside in a multisensory form, the brain processes this and comes up with (hopefully) an appropriate response. The scanning, testing, rejecting, and selecting amid countless alternatives happens with an immediacy that stops us being aware of the process itself.

It's so automatic that if you put this book down and stare at whatever scene is now in front of you – go on, do it – a whole landscape of colours, shapes, and sounds will immediately spring up in front of you without any apparent conscious intervention. Think: what did I do to create it?

You don't seem to *do* anything – it's all somehow *just there.* As if we have put on green sunglasses, everything appears green. The trouble is that the picture is constructed so instantly that we forget we have put the glasses on and that everything is being filtered through them.

An image that captures this memorably comes from an Irish policeman who would warn offenders off prison by saying:

> *'How would you like to spend 90 days in the land of striped sunshine?'*

If we're not careful, it's possible for us to spend 90 years this way, looking out through the bars of our own perceptions.

Let's explore perception further. If I give you the input 'Kodak', what do you see? People immediately make the connection to cameras, and some even see the yellow of the company's livery. This was a great problem for Kodak some years ago when they were trying to promote Kodak photocopiers. When the potential customer heard the name, their perceptual grid had a rich history of associations that stereotyped Kodak as merely a camera company. 'Thank you, we've plenty of film, no need to call,' was the immediate reflex response. People in most fields will testify how hard it is to change the perceptions of others. Like Pavlov's dogs, we become conditioned.

What's in a name? If I say to you, 'Personnel Department', I'm sure your grid immediately produces an association of highly underpaid people who do an invaluable job, should be promoted to the board tomorrow, and have their salary doubled. Or if I say to you, 'car salesperson', then quite clearly you see someone totally trustworthy, who you'd sign a blank cheque to now, and who you'd love your daughter to bring home. *No?*

Here it doesn't really matter what story you have in your grid. My point is that we have a large library of spontaneous associations, positive or negative, even when we just hear a name or label. Working with the tourist industry in Ireland recently (I love the idea of having whole countries, not just organizations and individuals, as clients), I tentatively tried the input that the English were actually highly misunderstood, passionate, and caring people in the countries they dominated in the past. Naturally, this led to a rather lively conversation, as several hundred years' worth of experience didn't quite match this proposition!

If we are to think more consciously, re-think, and re-interpret the world we see, it's necessary to be more aware of this matching process that our brains are doing for us thousands of times a day. We need to slow down or suspend the practice of making such selective judgements in order to allow fresh ways of seeing to become available to us.

As light travels at 700 million miles per hour, this 'slowing down' can't usually be in the mechanical sense of perception, but in the ways we interpret and think about the data we are getting into our brains. This is re-thinking.

However, 'getting' this idea intellectually is not enough to change the way we see things. Here's another visual experience – look at the image below. What is it?

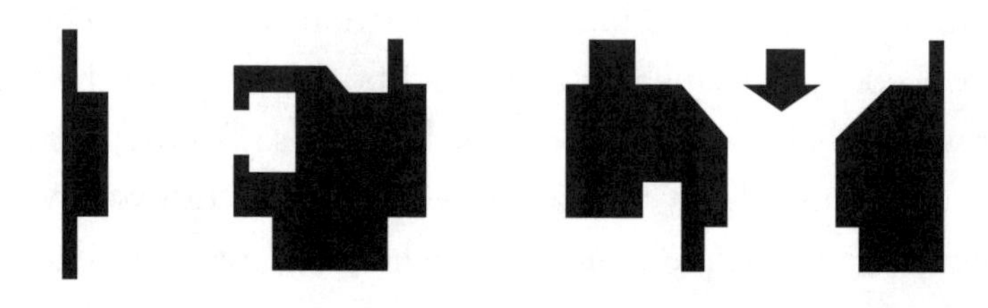

I've known it to take several hours for someone to decipher this. If you can't wait that long, the answer is at the bottom of the page.[1] The 'so what?' is that once our perceptual grid has noted an answer, it relaxes, takes this to be *the* answer, and stops looking for *even better solutions.*

Most people's initial perception is that there are many answers here – it could be pieces of machinery, a factory layout, a tap, or an arrow. But once what looks like the optimum solution clicks into place, the search for new ones is at an end. We have lost our perceptual 'virginity': notice how the longer you look at the image, the more difficult it is to return to your original, more open-ended view.

I call this the *problem of experience.* Once we have seen a good enough solution, it takes a lot of effort, courage, and brainpower to look for even better ways. For instance, if we have a fair forehand at tennis or a reasonable golf swing, our average ability can be more of an inhibitor to change than if we were rank beginners.

There is no such thing as a perfect solution, but there can be a more perfect search for solutions.

Our brain tends not to go through this search process if it doesn't seem to fit immediate survival needs. Over time we may develop more fixed ways of seeing things, which is why ageing has been described as a 'hardening of the categories'. We've labelled the problem, put it in a box, and stopped learning.

This should help us become a little more aware about the way we see things. Understanding ourselves has been described as pulling ourselves up by our own bootlaces. Brilliant neuroscientist Antonio Damasio describes the process of having only our own brains with which to understand ourselves as 'dizzying'.

---

[1] Fly.

Are we brainwashed?

We're all brainwashed to a degree. Not exactly in the ways used in wartime, ideological conditioning, interrogations, and cults, but in more subtle and insidious ways.

Don't believe it? Matthew Lieberman, a psychologist at the University of California, showed a research group photographs of black faces, all expressionless. In two-thirds of cases the brain's amygdala – often called the brain's panic button and responsible for our fight and flight response – was triggered. This was true for both black and white subjects, suggesting that social stereotypes are unconsciously picked up by us all, irrespective of what we might think consciously.

'Where Belief Is Born', Alok Jha, the *Guardian*, June 30, 2005.

Yet, self-awareness is a feature that more than anything distinguishes us from the instinctual nature of the animal kingdom. Biologist Julian Huxley described human nature as 'evolution become aware of itself'. It's just that our thinking process is so automatic and intimate to us that right from birth we have been thinking, while most of us have never stopped to consider what a thought is.

Let's see if you can intuitively capture the sense of *who* is doing all this perceiving, even just for a brief second.

Withdraw your mind from the words you've been reading on this page. Sit still and allow yourself to relax and become aware of the one who is doing the perceiving. Do you get just the vaguest sense that the person who is you, looking out at the world through your eyes, is the same person you have always been, throughout all the external changes in your body and surroundings?

This state of self-awareness can be explored more deeply through the practice of meditation, but even to reflect helps us to become aware how our inner perceptions condition us to the world we see.

Perceptions 'R' Us

The selective way we see things is conditioned by cultural as well as individual factors. The mind is primed to select certain messages over others.

Photograph: Joe Gerhardt

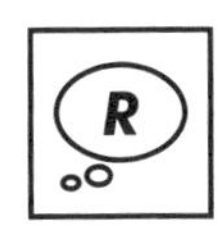

You've possibly glanced at the image from an English country church in the photograph above. Now cover it with your hand for a few seconds while you read on.

What did you see? Familiar and sad, isn't it? Or at least that's what almost everyone I've taken to view it says. We don't see it mindfully because we're so familiar with lists of war dead that we file it with similar impressions, and then move on.

I say 'we', but I'm assuming a certain kind of perception conditioned by European thinking and the experience of similar artefacts. A friend from Asia read it *as it is*, and was surprised at the way I and others had seen it. She had read clearly the last line that so many of us censor (you can remove your hand now!):

'All of whom by God's great mercy returned safely.'

Conventional perceptions

At a drinks party, Picasso was asked why he didn't paint people as they appeared. When he asked his questioner what his wife looked like in reality, he was shown a small, but lifelike portrait of a woman. 'Aha,' said Picasso, 'so your wife is only 12 inches tall?'

However, let's not jump to the conclusion that this automatic nature of perception is wholly bad. If we didn't 'edit' the sensory impressions we receive, then we'd never be able to act. Consciously trying to interpret every piece of data we receive would mean we simply couldn't perform actions that involve the firing of thousands or millions of electrical and chemical messages between the neurons of our brain – everyday tasks like making a cup of coffee, driving a car, or inserting a CD into the player. Most of the time our minds are usefully on autopilot.

Think of the experience of buying a new car. You look around the roads and what do you notice in the first few weeks of owning this vehicle? Suddenly the roads seem to be full of similar models. Or you come across a new word – for instance, *factotum*. Suddenly it's in every article you read, on television, overheard in conversation. Or your home town – Ashby-de-la-Zouch – is mentioned in a small piece in a newspaper. Immediately this leaps to the forefront of your awareness and you screen out what is objectively a much more important story.

You and I are unconsciously drawing the contours of our highly personalized maps of reality based on our own inner preoccupations, interests, and beliefs. In fact, we can reverse the everyday expression, 'seeing is believing', and re-think it as 'believing is seeing'.

Seeing only what you believe can be dangerous, as in the case of the South American peasants who had nothing in their mental 'grids' that matched with the sails of the Spanish invaders' ships. Because the sails were not in their database of memories, they didn't understand the approaching threat and returned to their farming. They saw, but they didn't believe.

A few hundred Spaniards were able to conquer large parts of a continent because the indigenous people had no perceptual tools to prepare them for the unfamiliar weaponry and organization of the invaders.

In a competitive setting, the 'sails' of some new, disruptive technology or upstart competitor are often invisible. The first response to the steam engine, the telephone, the internal combustion engine, the personal computer or the Internet was rejection. This blindness, or fear of the new, means that often leaders, heavily invested in yesterday's ideas, can miss the boat.

Seeing is believing?

After Queen Victoria visited London Zoo to have her first sight of a giraffe, she returned to the palace muttering, 'I still don't believe it.'

A champion of this narrow kind of perception was the chief engineer of the British Post Office, Sir William Preece, when he denied the value of the telephone in 1896. He said, *'The Americans have need of the telephone – but we do not. We have plenty of messenger boys.'*

Imagine my delight at presenting this quote to the senior management of a British telecommunications company. Their response was that unfortunately some of the same mindset still persisted 100 years later!

By now it should be clear that our mental map of the world is not the same thing as the real world we navigate through. 'The map is *not* the territory' is the central message of this chapter. There's an old military expression that says: 'If the map and the terrain differ, the terrain counts!'

Most of the time we are trying, for comfort's sake, to fit the world into our own map. While this works quite well in a literal sense for finding our way to the cinema or restaurant, in more complex areas of our lives it's about as accurate as old maps that say 'There be dragons here' or 'Large amounts of ocean omitted'.

Of course, just becoming aware of and changing our inner map doesn't necessarily amend the laws of physics in the outer world. Nor am I saying there is no such thing as objectivity. There is an apocryphal story about a group of Chinese philosophers who sat down on the banks of the Yangtze to discuss whether or not the river really existed. During their seminar, the river flooded and drowned them.

The three most important things we need to remember about the way we see things are:

- we see the world selectively: seeing what we expect to see and hearing what we expect to hear;
- our perceptions are based largely on past experience and conditioning; and
- We often mistake our perceptions, our map of the world, for *the* world, and assume that others are working from the same map.

What follows in the re-think section are ways of applying these insights to everyday situations.

RE-THINK NO. 1: BORROWING THE PERCEPTIONS OF OTHERS

Find an enthusiast

Tired, listless, lacking in passion? Sounds like an advert for a wonder pill, doesn't it? There are probably areas of your life that are important to you, but you have lost (or failed to ever find) passion for. In short, you need to re-think or refresh your perceptions.

I experienced this when I was doing my Bar exams in London. A tome on land law I was meant to master had a deceptively attractive cover of green, rolling fields, but inside revealed the full horror (to me) of the many sections of the Law of Property Act 1925, still a vital part of English property law. I was a man in search of a magic pill.

One night I was sitting in one of the four Inns of Court, Gray's Inn, where would-be barristers have to dine a certain number of nights to qualify. Eating dinner ranks up there with passing exams on this side of the legal profession. Two places to my left I overheard an American lady enthusing about the delights(!) of Land Law. At first I responded with the usual English attitude towards enthusiasm: either she's mad or she's selling something! She was explaining how the knowledge she had gained positively enriched her experience of walking through the streets of London. To know that this estate was leasehold, that one freehold, and so on, enabled her to understand more of the economic and social structure of her adopted country.

As the meal continued, I slowly realized that I had chosen a very negative response to my work, and merely *perceiving* it as a chore was also holding me back. It wasn't so much a case of 'glass half full, glass half empty' – I was off this particular scale and complaining to myself that nobody had even given me a glass!

Where's my glass?

We often talk about 'glass half full or half empty', but it's clear that there's a third position: 'nobody even gave me a glass.'

Now, I won't pretend that I was born again and that I'd enthusiastically choose law books over a good erotic thriller, but it was as if a small button in my brain had been pressed. From then on I found myself making a choice to approach my studies with greater positivity. If someone else was finding fascination in all this, then it was my loss not to discover at least some relevance and interest.

I never spoke to this lady to thank her, but this small insight has become a big driver in my life. I'm continually seeking out those who are passionate about a topic, even if I can't see it, and avoiding the company of those who are nay-sayers, the 'no glass at all' community.

Re-thinking enthusiasm

Language can limit or expand our grid. To re-think often means to re-visit the real meaning of words that we use without awareness. *Enthusiasm* is originally from the Greek, *en – theos. In god.* There is something spiritual about being touched by the enthusiasm or passion of another, even if it's learning Norwegian, double-entry bookkeeping, or the transport history of your country (three topics that don't immediately fill me with joy!). You *can* find an enthusiast. You choose.

Overhear conversations in a restaurant or on the bus and you will be aware of a low level of grumbling, people indulging in the do-it-yourself therapy of criticizing others: their colleagues, their boss, family, and even partner. It's a seductively easy track in your grid to become locked into, but *you do have a choice*!

> *Avoid this company and find – either personally, in your reading, or over the net – those who are most excited by life or enthusiastic about a particular topic, especially one you're stuck on.*

Enthusiasm is contagious. It's the magic bullet you need if your batteries are running down.

A visitor's perception

We all know that a visitor to our town or country may quickly become more knowledgeable about the place than the inhabitants. Quite simply, they are seeing so much that locals take for granted.

> *Why not adopt this visitor's viewpoint for ourselves and ask as many visitors as possible for their views of your culture, history, or surroundings?*

As our house frequently welcomes visitors from overseas, I always make a habit of asking them about their perceptions of Oxford or England. A Chinese professor who stayed with us said that what struck him most was seeing so many old people on the streets, alone.

A friend from Nepal told me it was very clear what was different: our obsession with sex – on television, in newspapers, advertisements. Although intellectually I understand this, the ubiquity of these images dulls the mind to how prevalent they are.

But he also observed the much greater opportunities for women in the UK compared with the country regions of Nepal where females are not generally expected to receive a full education.

One way we can play the role of the visitor is by priming our mind to notice certain patterns around us. A famous photographer's first instruction to a group he was coaching was 'to photograph everything yellow'. Strangely, narrowing your perception in this way can allow you to see certain objects and connections more intensely.

Alternatively, you could prime your mind to look for changes that have happened in your surroundings in the last five years, the first signs of the new season, or the relative happiness of faces you pass in the street.

It's amazing how much keener and fresher your perceptions are when you set your mind to focus narrowly instead of on the usual landscape view.

Observing the same thing, taking off our own perceptual glasses, we may be seeing the same territory, but *noticing* completely different features, which mean something unique to us. What we're blind to is the six billion plus other ways of perceiving the world. Curiosity about the way different cultures see things opens the mind like nothing else.

Seeing things differently

A recent study at the University of Michigan compared the way that North American and Chinese students paid attention to photographs by tracking their eye movements. Researchers Richard Nisbett and Hannah-Faye Chua observed that the Oriental view was to take in the whole context and background of the picture, while the

Americans (of European extraction) focused far more on the detail in the foreground.

Nisbett concludes that 'They (Asians) literally are seeing the world differently ... they live in a more socially complicated world than we do. They have to pay more attention to others than we do. We are individualists.'

Worthwhile (www.worthwhilemag.com)
'Seeing Things Differently – Literally',
Curt Rosengren, 23 August 2005.

To bring this closer to home, one of the great culture gaps is between parents and children. You could certainly test the openness of your 'grid' by *facing up to your children's music.* If you think that you are not subject to any narrowing of perceptions, just consider the age at which you responded like your parents did to new music. It's when you find yourself saying:

- Is that really music?
- Why is it so angry and loud?
- I can't hear the words.
- I bet they can't play live!

The moment comes sooner than we think. We may believe that in many areas of our lives we are extremely tolerant of the new, and just make an exception to our general open-mindedness when we hear certain forms of music. *This is the thin end of the wedge in terms of the mind closing.*

Try listening to and discussing – as much as possible without judging – your children's music. Right now I'm enjoying Muse and Sigur Rós ...

Finally, we can borrow the perceptions of another by tuning into an enthusiast who is also an expert. Walking the countryside with a friend who has specialist knowledge of English landscape architecture, I realized she perceives both the present and the past in what to me are just fields. And spending time with a passionate man who lectures on opera, I'm able to 'borrow' his perceptions long enough to enrich my own understanding of music I'm largely ignorant about.

These opportunities are all around us, but they require us to slow down and readjust our perceptions just long enough to allow new influences in. A visitor's or an enthusiast's mindset is a fresh one, excited by the search for new experiences and knowledge. Make this mindset yours.

RE-THINK NO. 2: NEW FANTASIES, NEW HEROES

New fantasies

There are probably fantasies in the attic of your mind that you could do with dusting down. Some of these can still be fun to play with – I am able to rehearse scoring a hat-trick for the England football team while simultaneously knowing that it's not going to happen.

However, fantasies that we can turn into reality are much more useful, particularly in the second half of life. Swiss psychologist Carl Jung likened this transition in life to turning over a tapestry or bedspread: the reverse side may not be so vibrant, but it can be more rich and fascinating.

Here we can use the power of selective perception to positive effect.

I was coaching a businessman who told me that one of his fantasies since childhood was to learn to play the piano. We talked about why this was so important to him, and just let the idea sit in his mind.

Two weeks later he rang me to say that he had seen an advertisement in a local newspaper for a second-hand piano, had bought it, and was already having his second lesson. A year later we spoke again and he described how he was getting up half an hour earlier to play and loving every minute of it.

This is a fantasy that he *could* have pursued at any time in his life, but because our conversation brought it to the forefront of his mind, he had 'set' himself to notice the opportunity in a paper he read every week.

We could say that this is just a hobby rather than a fantasy. But for him it's more than a pastime. The richness of the experience, of sitting at his piano and hearing music in his head far beyond the level at which he's playing, is a living fantasy.

> *So, what are your 'phantom hobbies', the things that you've always seen yourself doing if only you had time? Pick one and look for the opportunity to start it now.*

And, of course, your fantasies may also be about places that you really want to visit and experiences you've always dreamed of having. There's never been a time, particularly in the Western world, when the gap or barrier between having a desire and fulfilling it is so small, if only we can convince ourselves to begin.

What do you give to someone who has everything? It's usually not a thing, but an *experience*. For his sixtieth birthday a friend's wife arranged a trek for him and his two sons in the Himalayas instead of the usual party. These are not well-off people, but there's usually a creative way of fixing these things. So don't watch on TV – or read about – the '40 things to do before you die' – the trick is to make the experiences come alive for you.

These are fun, or life-enriching activities, but sometimes your fantasies are bigger.

A skinny 12-year-old swimmer told his coach that he wanted to win Olympic Gold, probably in breaststroke. Instead of ridiculing him, the coach took him literally, and helped him with a practical philosophy of 'breaking down the dream'. In other words, setting him milestones that worked backward from the dream in achievable stages. This month you'll have to be doing this speed, next month you'll have to put in this much training, and so on.

The swimmer in question was Adrian Moorhouse, who won Olympic Gold in 1988. He had the same coach from the day of his fantasy to becoming the best in the world. There's an interesting coda to this story: his coach can't swim.

A remarkable example of breaking down the impossible into manageable slices is the survival story of mountaineer Joe Simpson, told in the film *Touching The Void.* He crawled down 19,000 feet of an Andean mountain with the most horrendous injuries. Extraordinarily, he attributes much of his survival to an almost valueless watch he got at a French service station. With this, he broke down his tortuous decent into 20-minute intervals because the big picture was just too impossible to conceive. He would aim to reach a nearby rock or overhang in these 20-minute epochs – if he did it in 18, he was elated, in 23 and he was really angry with himself.

Now here it was a matter of life or death: Joe's motivation was just to reach a position where his body would be found after his certain death. But we can apply this same thinking to the great things we'd like to experience or achieve while we are still alive, never being afraid to set our sights high, but having the wisdom to break it down into manageable stages.

What's the first manageable stage of the fantasy that you want to make real?

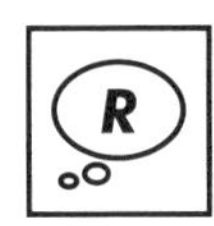

It's hard to use the word fantasy today without many people assuming you mean sex. One of the cleverest re-thinks on this subject comes from a very unusual source, Rabbi Shmuel Boteach. His provocative book, *A Jewish Guide To Adultery*,[2] is actually a guide to having the same level of passion with your wife as you would have with a mistress. Quirky maybe, but it's a wonderful idea from a man I know to be intensely spiritual behind his alter ego as a TV rabbi. And you don't have to be Jewish to learn from it.

New heroes for old

Most of us have heroes, heroines, or role models from whom we gain inspiration. They may be historical, alive or dead, famous or known to us. But what role have they played recently in helping you to lead the creative, successful, or passionate life you know you should be leading? Like the interests we put on our CV, which we now don't have time to enjoy, our list of heroes may be past their sell-by date.

Who your heroes are and why they have had such an impact upon you is a fascinating discussion to have with your partner, friends, or possibly even a mentor.

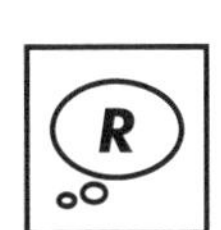

Very often you will find that this is like holding up a mirror to your own life – or at least your life as you would wish it to be. My own icons tend to be mavericks, outsiders, innovators. People like Richard Thompson, Gene Clark, Natalie Merchant, Gary Snyder, Gaudi, and Erik Satie.

---

[2] Rabbi Shmuel Boteach, *The Jewish Guide to Adultery: How to Turn Your Marriage into an Illicit Affair*, Pan Paperback, 1995.

So why not (a) look more deeply into the lives, achievements, and wisdom of those who you would list as your existing heroes, and (b) find at least one new one?

Have you ever had the fantasy of writing? Most people have. My new hero and guiding light in this respect is a Frenchman, Jean-Dominique Bauby. He wrote an extraordinarily observant book, *The Diving Bell and the Butterfly*. Bauby, who was a *bon viveur* and editor-in-chief of French magazine *Elle*, was suddenly plunged at age 43 into a locked-in syndrome where the only organ he could move was his left eye. His mind was alive, but nothing else. He dictated his brilliant book by blinking his left eye different number of times to indicate each letter or punctuation point. He died of a heart attack on 19 March 1997, two days after his book was published.

Jacket cover from *The Diving Bell and the Butterfly: A Memoir of Life in Death* by Jean-Dominique Bauby. Used by permission of Alfred A. Knopf, a division of Random House.

I keep a copy of this book at my writing table. If I ever think I have 'writer's block', this new hero of mine puts things clearly into perspective.

A re-think on history is that its true value is not in reading about the rise and fall of governments, wars, religions, kings and queens, but in drawing inspiration from the lives of remarkable people. This gives us a better opportunity of inventing a more successful future for ourselves and those around us. The notion that by understanding history we can prevent ourselves from repeating it is patently nonsense. Perhaps we've been dwelling too much on the history of failure rather than the acts of greatness, genius, or mould-breaking creativity.

We should have the study of Creative Minds as a module on every degree course.

RE-THINK NO. 3: SPRING-CLEAN YOUR BELIEFS

Our memories and beliefs are not changeable at will. They live an ephemeral existence in the synapses, or gaps, between the neurons of our brains. But they condition what we notice and pay attention to.

So, in order to think differently, imagine spring-cleaning your beliefs. This means exposing them to the air, sometimes for the first time. It may also mean realizing that some of the beliefs you carried around with you for years are no longer true for you. A very brave form of re-thinking is to admit to yourself or others that you have simply been wrong. It must have taken a great deal of courage for physicist Stephen Hawking to admit to his peers at a conference that he had been wrong in his beliefs about black holes. Wrong for several decades.

Having more creative conversations with others is the starting point. Too often an 'exchange of views' means taking our prejudices for a walk, polishing them up by speaking to someone sensible (i.e. someone like me!), then settling them down for a good nap in their comfortable nests.

A creative conversation means *we are prepared to test our beliefs and opinions, ideally with someone with a different mindset.* So, take a risk, talk to a stranger.

By exposing ourselves to other minds, through discussion or reading material we wouldn't normally tackle, we can go deeper into our own perceptions by trying to understand what our partner, our colleague, or even our organization really *believes* in.

Ask your mother, partner, or friend what they believe about the big questions: the purpose of life, what happens after death, God or not-God, the true value of education, whether we choose our parents, and so on.

Smit's Eden Creed

'I say to people when they work here that they've got to say hello to 20 people every day, read a book that they never normally read, and then discuss it, cook a meal for all the people who make it worth-while going to work, make someone else's wishes come true.'

Tim Smit, founder of the Eden Project,
world-famous ecological attraction in the UK

My experience is that you'll be surprised, fascinated, or even a little alarmed when you start this level of conversation. Being alarmed can be a positive sign that you're on the way to thinking differently. When people use the phrase 'I'm not comfortable with that', I'm often tempted to respond, 'Well you damn well shouldn't be – change isn't comfortable.'

Beliefs are deeper than values. The illustration, 'The belief iceberg', portrays how our beliefs and opinions underlie our values and actions.

I discovered that a friend believes that we have more than one life. This means that he *values* nature and all other life forms, perhaps because he's sensitive to what life form he'll return in! This translates into behaving with kindness and being passionate about hospitality to strangers and guests.

THE BELIEF ICEBERG

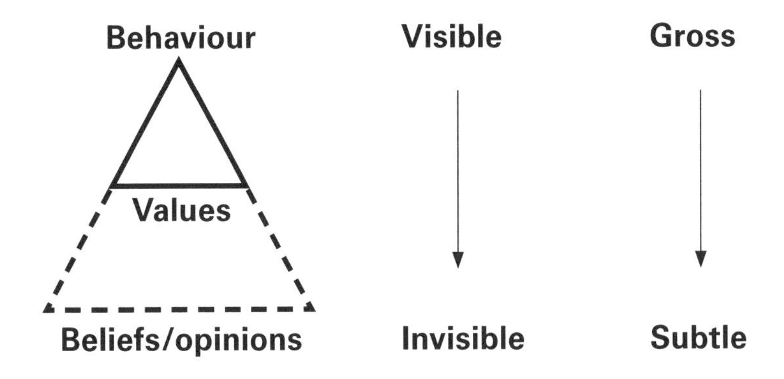

Sometimes the connection between these levels may seem tenuous, but let me give you a practical example from my role as a business speaker and coach.

Lexus in the UK and Europe is one of my clients. When it first entered the US car market, almost no one gave it a chance of competing with the other luxury marques, in particular Mercedes and BMW. But in a few short years it was outselling these much-admired rivals, and for over a decade won the coveted J D Power Customer Satisfaction Award.

Much of this success came from the level of belief. Eiji Todo, the visionary behind the birth of Lexus, championed the *belief* that a more perfect luxury car could be built, that Lexus could win the competitive race, and that its pursuit of perfection could be stepped up to a new level over and over again. The first model had *hundreds* of new patents, and the belief in silence and smooth running translated into the experience that a Lexus engine could be run at 120 mph with a glass of champagne on the body of the car without spilling a drop.

This belief in a better way, one that represented the best aspects of Japanese life (today call the J-factor), naturally translates into Lexus *values* such as 'Treat the customer as a guest in your own home'. Taking this seriously and moving up the iceberg, you could hardly fail to *behave* in a way that delivered the best levels of customer care that knocks the socks off the competition. It works!

Beliefs give birth to values, which in turn guide behaviour. If you're in an organization, forget value statements – most lists of them are indistinguishable – go deeper and begin with *beliefs*. The same applies to your personal life.

Starter questions are:

- Why do we/I believe we/I can contribute something better, different and more valuable to the world?
- Why are we/I in this role or job?
- What do we/I believe about human nature?
- What do we/I believe is the purpose of an organization?

I'm recommending that you make space and time in your life, not for small talk, but for big talk. For deeper conversations with yourself, those close to you and your professional acquaintances.

In this way you will be spontaneously holding up a mirror to your own deeper beliefs to see which ones are still valid, and which need to be thrown out in a spring-clean.

Too much small talk – not enough *Big Talk*!

Understandably, such a creative conversation may feel a little embarrassing at first, even if you're just having it with yourself. A way of limbering up is to start with something lighter: what do you or the person you are talking with believe in that's a little 'weird'? I can assure you that even contenders for Mr or Ms Rational Man or Woman believe something strange, perhaps something they've never told anyone before. It may be that Elvis is still alive (didn't you know?), or that they have been abducted by aliens. Then you can laugh, relax, and automatically your mind is opened up to exploring further, to enquiring within.

Someone I asked gave the surprising and poignant answer that he believed, or chose to believe, that his father, who died when he was 12, was still alive. He would often look for him in a crowd or at any time he was out and about. Of course, he knew rationally that his father was dead. But even after 50 years he continued to look for him, finding comfort in the belief he would see him again. He's not crazy – he's a very well adjusted and practical engineer.

Why not visit beliefs early on in a relationship? When people make pre-nuptial arrangements they focus on the surface, material level of life, but isn't it more important to exchange what you believe to be the purpose of the relationship, the role of children, and what you think will bring you both the greatest degree of happiness? A lot of future grief might be reduced if this can be done in a thoughtful way.

I draw a line at copying the famous writer who claims to have drawn up a mission statement for his family on his wedding day. But starting the conversation, or the Big Talk, *now* is important. Time for a spring-clean.

re-think two

Awakening curiosity

Our ability to be curious is dependent upon wonder, on not taking the everyday for granted. It's easy to become blind to the beauty that's outside your window, whether you are looking from your living room, a train, or a plane. I'm amazed to see business travellers on an airplane reading the *Financial Times* when the setting sun is a ball of fire above mountains of clouds as far as the eye can see.

Exploring the road less travelled in your mind creates the mental space for new solutions to emerge. If we think in tramlines, we miss so much.

To wonder means to appreciate life more fully. If we lose this sense, we're barely alive, or at least alive to fresh possibilities. But being bombarded with so much information may have stretched our ability to wonder so far that it has lost its elasticity or bounce. In a recent television series about the oceans of the world, naturalist David Attenborough and his team discovered new species unknown to anyone on earth. Yet I found myself thinking, 'Well, I always knew there were plenty of fish in the sea.'

In a similar vein, I love the story of the elderly lady who had never seen the ocean. A helpful young man drove her to the seaside, where she stood and watched the tide coming in for ten minutes before shaking her head and saying, 'Is that all it does?'

Never mind compassion fatigue – we have 'Wonder Fatigue'. This happens to any sense when faced with overload: 100 billion neurons in the brain? Just telephone numbers (though I'd like to see you load a number that long into your Nokia!). An image that captures this for me is an advertisement for a hair product where Hollywood actress Jennifer Aniston flicks her hair, winks at us, and says, 'Here comes the science', as if to say, let's allow these strange little men in white coats to tell you some incredible things about the product for a nano-second, but really it's better not to wonder – just look at *me*!

So here comes the science. I'm going to present you with some data.

Don't just scan down the list – allow yourself the space and time to reflect on any of the items that stretch your mind. Go for a walk and just let the notion play in your mind, or discuss what it means to you with a friend or your children.

Set any cynicism aside: that's fine for demolishing ideas, but here I suggest you flex your ability to wonder, to allow your mind to visualize pictures beyond the numbers.

- There are 100 billion stars in our galaxy.

- There are over 200 billion galaxies (in the observable universe).

- The solid matter we see is completely insubstantial; we are 99.5 per cent space.

- Today's most sophisticated super-computers, which process multi-billions of bits per second, pale by comparison to the human brain's unconscious data processing capabilities.

- Atoms are not things – just tendencies.

- The universe is expanding at an ever-increasing rate (but feel how solid the ground seems under your feet).

- You now have in your body more than a million of the atoms that were once in the body of Jesus Christ, George Harrison, Gandhi or Mother Teresa.

- Of all the atoms in your body, 98 per cent are replaced within a year = new body!

- We share 96 per cent of our DNA with a chimpanzee, and half the banana genome is also found in the human genome. And we have 85 per cent in common with zebra fish.

It shouldn't be difficult to take the notion from *Alice In Wonderland* and believe three impossible things before breakfast – they are all around us.

These aren't insights we can simply act on. If the world is hurtling through space at great speed, rotating on its axis as it goes, this knowledge doesn't mean we should hold on tighter. But it can awaken our sense of wonder that we are here at all, alive at a time when our scientific instruments can explore so deeply into space, the depths of the ocean or the furthest reaches of our planet.

If you didn't experience some expansion of your mind when you read the items above, I'd be very surprised. What awakens our sense of curiosity is the very fact that we have the ability to contemplate, explore and reflect upon the meaning of these findings.

The deepest mystery – and the one that science with its outward looking eyes has had least success in unravelling – is the nature of consciousness itself. Captain Kirk might have said in his log, '*Inner* Space – the final frontier.' Winston Churchill was prescient when he observed that 'the empires of the future are the empires of the mind.'

Unravelling the secrets of consciousness is, of course, well beyond the scope of this, or probably any, book. The rest of this chapter is concerned with practical ways in which we can awaken curiosity about ourselves and others. It begins with wondering.

Re-discovering why

Einstein said it was amazing after a formal education that anybody has any curiosity left. This is encapsulated in the statement 'one month in a job and you go blind', said to me once by a client.

When I ask a group what it means, they readily respond that we soon become part of the furniture, that the systems and routines of work rob us of freshness of thought, and we learn to accept things the way they are.

Of course, one month is arbitrary. For some people it's three days. For the first three days in a new situation they are at least *thinking* the difficult, awkward questions. 'Why do we do it like this?' 'What's that system *for*?' 'What does he actually *do*?' The last of these questions is likely to get you into great trouble, but at least you are seeing the situation with a fresh eye rather than sinking into unquestioning acceptance.

The trouble is that by the time you have enough authority to act on these provocative questions, you may have become part of the problem yourself.

The natural mind-opener is the trusty question 'why?' As we know, children use this all the time. After the third 'why', you might as well buy them chocolate because you don't know the answer yourself. But you can usefully apply this strategy to the topic you are now thinking about.

Bring your mind to it and ask at least three 'whys' about the essential nature of your task. Allow your mind to explore where these take you, and capture the ideas on paper.

At least one successful entrepreneur has run his whole business through the power of continually asking 'why' in an obsessive, naïve, and child-like way. Ricardo Semler manages Semco in Brazil on this principle. Originally a manufacturing company, this several-hundred-million-dollar-turnover business has transformed itself from manufacturing into IT, property, and services because every few months people in the business sit down and ask themselves *why* are we in this particular business – and why not in this one? They then steer the business accordingly and in the process have become almost inflation-proof: 27 per cent annual growth over the last 20 years in the rollercoaster ride that is the Brazilian economy tells its own story.

What impresses me most in conversation with this quietly spoken and relaxed man is how the curious use of 'why' has helped to transform his working practices in a way that most large organizations hope to achieve merely by the production of bland mission and value statements. Workers at Semco can choose 11 different ways of getting paid. (Why not?) It's the workers who employ other workers and set their salaries. (Why not?) And the reality is that they are at least as tough as 'management', a concept that barely exists at Semco.

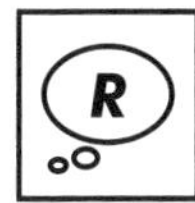

Why not 'retire a little'?

It's clear that our fixed view of employment as starting early in life and continuing until we retire is due for a major rethink. The times in one's life when we have less income, we probably have better health, and vice versa. In Semco, people are able to make arrangements with colleagues so that at certain critical points of their family or personal life they can work less and get paid less without affecting their long-term prospects in the company.

This is a striking example of how life can be enriched by being creatively curious about what most people take for granted. Albert Einstein's observation that he wasn't necessarily more intelligent than others in his field – as evidenced by his average school grades – but that he was more intensely *curious* about what made the universe work is a clarion call to awaken the curiosity gene in all of us.

Curiosity and the new

I'm amazed how often I can sit at dinner with people I haven't met and find out a great deal about their life, passions, and beliefs without them even learning the basics about me. When I was in my 20s people would ask me at a drinks party what I did. I would say that I trained as a barrister, but was now teaching Transcendental Meditation as a way to help people manage stress and become more creative. After some throat-clearing, I would then be asked, 'Er ... What branch of the law did you specialize in?' This is a blind spot we all share, screening out the unfamiliar.

It doesn't have to be this way. While the mind has a tendency to close down, and lead to aging as a more fixed way of seeing things, people who keep their minds active needn't show the expected decline.

People who are interested in others are themselves more interesting.

What holds us back from discovering more about others is the tendency for us to mingle with and have conversation with people who are sensible, balanced and with refined judgement. People just like … me!

It's the same with our personal tastes. If you go into a music shop (or – just as likely these days – log on to iTunes) do you muse, 'I'll have a look and see what's new here in Urban or World Music?' Or do you think 'I'll just look for the familiar sections I'm used to' – 'Do they have that re-master of *Groundhogs Live at the Marquee* c. 1971?'

Do a John Peel

The late great DJ John Peel said that he would always listen to something he hadn't heard rather than something he already knew. Now while this curiosity meant he admired music that a lot of his original fan base had trouble with, it does show a curiosity for the novel and the untried, which is at the heart of creativity. It certainly helped him to 'reinvent' his career over and over again.

When was the last time you tried to expand your tastes – literary, artistic, musical or scientific – to discover something really fresh and new? Or are you stuck with the mindset 'I know what I like'?

Next time you go looking for music – or books or films – add something new to the familiar that you are putting in your basket.

Questioning assumptions

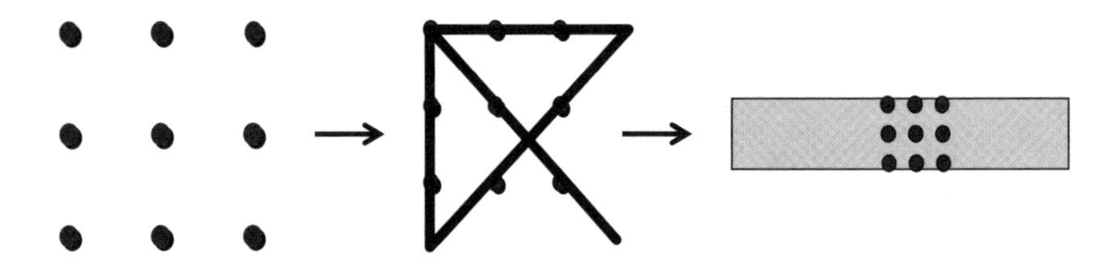

There comes a stage in every book on creativity when you're going to be exhorted to 'think outside the box'. Not here! I believe it's a very limiting expression. When I'm asked to help a group of people to think outside the box, I usually respond, 'What box?' If I'm speaking to someone saturated in management-speak, words like 'paradigm' and 'mindset' will appear, but often people will say, 'You know what I mean'. 'You know what I mean' is a phrase reserved in English for when we have no idea how to articulate something. We are often not curious about the box we're in because it is simply too close and intimate to be visible to us.

Look at the old puzzle of how to join nine dots in the configuration of three lines of three dots, with four straight lines, without the pen leaving the paper. Most people these days have seen the second answer in the box above. The idea is that all you have to do is think outside the box and then hey, presto, a solution comes to you. I suggest that you throw out of the window any book that only has the four-line solution in it because it seems that only authors of books on creativity are unable to think beyond this solution!

Let's think more deeply, and with greater curiosity, about this problem.

Given the four-line solution, most people, if asked 'who said you couldn't go outside the 9 dots?' would reply 'nobody'. In fact, this is wrong in a subtly dangerous way. If we couldn't think of a solution it was because *our own mind had set a limiting rule.* It had made a number of assumptions. That's why the third solution – joining all 9 dots with *one* straight line – is all the more interesting.

This answer was sent by a nine-year-old girl to a famous innovator, Professor James Adams at Stanford University. He had worked on NASA moon projects, but the power of this girl's solution took him aback. It really knocks the socks off a four-line one because it challenges a number of assumptions. Firstly, of course, the idea that you can re-think or redefine the puzzle itself. More specifically it challenges assumptions about:

- thickness of the line
- type of writing apparatus
- closeness of the dots
- what 'joining' means
- the definition of the problem itself: for instance that you could only do it with four lines.

Perhaps the biggest one of all is still missed: the assumption that the puzzle has to be set in two dimensions.

So what? By challenging assumptions, we are able to create many new solutions. In fact, there is probably no limit to the number of four-line, three-line, two-line or, if you really want to push out the boundaries, *no line* solutions that still fit within the basic instructions given. If some of this feels a bit like cheating, then you know you are on the leading edge of innovation – if *I* do it, it's innovation; if *someone else* does it, it's cheating.

To foster curiousity it helps to revisit aspects of a problem or a situation with a childlike and more open view. Naturally we need to marry this with adult experience. Child*like* does not mean child*ish.*

I often introduce the creative process by asking people to think about something in their life or work that needs a creative solution. Then simply to go on a walk with another person who will help them to think of two or three assumptions that they are making.

The usual response to assumptions being challenged by another is denial – our mental grid is defensive in protecting its familiar territory, like a mother tiger protecting her cubs. Our fixed patterns of thought come with strong emotions attached. But when people return to the topic later in the day, almost inevitably they see some small tear is opening in what seemed like an impenetrable shield around the problem. Occasionally some have a genuine *eureka*, but I regard this as a bonus at this stage.

Among the most common of assumptions that hold us back is the view that someone else won't listen to our request – for instance, assignment to a new job project, a fresh arrangement over child access, etc. Past failure may have worn this channel in the brain into a deep ravine from which little light can escape, so we won't even make the request in a convincing way. It's already been shot down inside our own mind, and in this way the assumption fulfils its own prophecy.

Thinking 'why not?' and 'what if?'

The very words we use to define a topic carry with them a set of assumptions with its own DNA of associations. For instance, if I ask individuals to draw a chair, 9 times out of 10 they will come up with something that looks like this.

A more curious mind may hear the word, but not be limited by commonplace associations with it. Look, for instance, at the picture below of the surprisingly comfortable seat created in the 1970s by a Norwegian designer, Peter Opsvik. Many people find this more comfortable because the weight of the body is supported in different positions rather than just being focused on the base of the spine.

Balans Variable chair reproduced with kind permission of Peter Opsvik (Design), Stokke (manufacturer).

'Skyscraper' is another word whose fixed associations are being broken by architects like Daniel Liebeskind. A new computer simulation for an office park in Milan shows his acrobatically curving tower together with a torqued, muscular one from Zaha Hadid, flanked by what seems to be an impossibly slim wafer shape from architect Isozaki. Everywhere we look in the field of design, fixed and expected patterns are being challenged.

Listening to your children can be a great source of ideas. This can be true even of teenagers – now dubbed 'screenagers' – who think that the screen is real and that parents are virtual. We know they have a value as the family technology butler, and …

… it's a useful re-think to have a 13-year-old give feedback on, for instance, your website and how the family uses technology. But you can also ask them for career advice if you really tune in openly to what they say.

A few years ago I was travelling too much and not seeing enough of my son. 'I know you think I work too hard, Jamie,' I said. Having the precise mind that he does, he mulled this over for a moment, and said, 'No, Dad, you don't work too *hard* – you work too *much*.' This subtle difference has been one of the most useful pieces of career advice I've received, and has helped me to re-focus my business on fewer bigger events and less of the more time-consuming, albeit rewarding, ones I used to say yes to.

When we hear, or more likely half-hear, an idea we want to shut out, we have a ready armoury of words with which to deal the deathblow. For simplicity's sake, I shorthand this as 'yes, but' thinking.

The most common expressions people use to 'yes, but' an idea they have probably judged too quickly are:

- With respect …
- With greatest respect …
- I hear what you say, but …
- I see your point, but …
- It's all right in theory, but …

Of course, these all mean essentially the same thing – 'no' to the fresh, unfamiliar or new avenues of thought. It's not the words, but the underlying attitude of challenging something new before we've had a chance to explore it that is so damaging to creativity. Although I do quite like the academics' response to the last one, which is to say, 'It works in *practice* … but I don't like the *theory*.'

Of course, when other people 'yes, but' we can laugh at them, but it's not something you or I participate in. Or is it? Just catch yourself out over the next two days 'yes, butting' (sometimes silently, but it's the same thing) the suggestions of family members, work colleagues, or ideas you come across in the paper and on the radio.

> *When you sit down with your partner, you of course always say 'why not?' or 'what if?' to all of their suggestions for the weekend. Or do you?*

I don't mean to remove your whole vocabulary, or to say that 'yes, but' is never appropriate. It does have a place as a gatekeeper and sanity check on our zanier ideas. However, the shock of discovering how often we 'yes, but' and therefore limit our curiosity is very sobering.

The 'yes, but' box

Sometimes we need simple reminders. For this reason, I've often used the 'yes, but' box at creative sessions, and suggested that every time someone 'yes, buts', it incurs a 1 euro/dollar/pound fine. And for the person who 'yes, buts' the idea of the 'yes, but' box I usually ask for a 5 euro contribution!

An innovative team from a bank I worked with recently thought that after one session with the box they got the idea and no longer needed it. They were serious, intelligent people and it seemed a little silly. Their boss described to me how, for the next hour, their thinking sunk into a swamp of 'yes, buts', and they immediately resurrected the box. Old habits die hard, and most of the time we don't know that we are 'yes, butting'.

Thinking 'why not?' or 'what if?' is a discipline that requires practice. All around us are role models that demonstrate the corrosive influence of too much 'yes, butting' – for instance, the oppositional nature of politics and legal arguments. When I worked for a well-known television company, it became clear to me that there were only four interview questions commonly deployed:

- Yes, but …
- But isn't there a danger that …?
- But aren't you really trying to say …?
- Won't people find a difficulty/danger/concern/problem (insert any other negative word here) with your argument that …?

No wonder that the interviewee becomes more defensive and fights back with knee-jerk answers. It's less common for us to think in the more creative vein of 'why not?' or 'what if?' It requires a suspension of the faculty we rate too highly – our ability to judge. This is why it takes courage to be curious about an idea long enough to explore it, play with it, and just entertain what would happen 'if …'

Many great ideas – from the steam engine to the Internet – have been 'yes, butted' most virulently by experts who have the most invested in the old ways of thinking and working. Even His Nerdship himself, William Gates III, initially 'yes, butted' the economic potential of the Internet, but to his credit did an amazing U-turn in the 1990s.

Spend half an hour on what new developments in your own field you have 'yes, butted' as fringe or peripheral. It can open up a whole universe of new possibilities.

RE-THINK NO. 4: OPEN-PAGE THINKING

You'll remember the line 'one month in a job and you go blind'. What's required to counter this is a more open-minded and curious approach: Open-Page thinking. We can apply this not just to our work, but also to our life and relationships. This is inspired by the concept of the beginner's mind in the Japanese Zen tradition: 'In the beginner's mind there are many possibilities, in the expert's there are few.'[1]

To practice Open-Page thinking means approaching a situation with the freshness of a beginner *and* the experience of someone who knows the problem well. Here's how to start.

Teach yourself ignorance

I'd love to run this as a two-day seminar! As adults, we pretend we know the answers to many things we are ignorant about. Appearing at least a little omniscient in one's own field makes us feel good. Although the *idiot savant* has a place in popular culture – Forrest Gump, for example – approaching the familiar as if we were beginners is often not a comfortable position to adopt.

Consider this: a friend or colleague mentions to you a film, a book, a report in your own area of professional interest and asks you if you know it. How often do you say, 'Well, yes, not in great detail', while actually thinking 'what the hell is she talking about?' This can occur several times a week: it's your mind shutting down and saying that you already know this, don't need to know it, or perhaps just need to pretend so that you won't be sneered at.

The next time this happens, try admitting your ignorance to let fresh material into your mind.

For instance, if it's a report, ask them for a brief summary. There are two potential advantages to this. The first is that it might save you having to read the damn thing. The second is that you may find that they haven't read it either!

---

[1] Suzuki-roshi (1905-71), Japanese Zen priest.

Teaching yourself ignorance really means admitting, first to yourself and then to others, that the knowledge you have of a particular problem or situation is provisional or limited. Most of us believe we know more than we do. This is why so much creativity and innovation comes from what we could call 'tutored ignorance'.

When the entrepreneur Richard Branson started his airline Virgin Atlantic, he approached it with Open-Page thinking, a healthy dose of ignorance in that he knew nothing about running an airline. However, he did have the more uncluttered, curious mind of someone who knew only too well what it was like to be a *customer* of an airline, and therefore was prone to thinking '*What if* it were entertaining for the customer?' '*Why not* have an on-board masseuse?' This freshness of perception enabled him to create one of the best customer experiences in the world.

He also applied Open-Page thinking by making a practice of hiring people who did not have a background in the airline industry. Except the pilots.

Virgin's other great re-think that has spawned many copiers is their policy of recruiting for attitude first, skills second. You can train for skills, but changing attitudes is far harder.

Fire yourself!

Applying the concept of Open-Page thinking to our own lives involves standing back from our daily preoccupations.

What if you were to fire yourself from your daily work, company or even family and spend some time entertaining the daring thoughts:

- What if I wasn't working for this department/school/organization? What creative changes would I make?

- What if I was starting this relationship afresh? What would I now do differently?

The idea of firing yourself has been used successfully in business by one of the founders and previous chief executives of Intel, Andy Grove, who every year would say to his senior team that they and he were fired for a day. They would travel to a fresh venue outside work, look back at their company and think, 'Now we're fired and don't work for Intel any more, what would we change?'

Apparently these sessions were incredibly creative. Even if it's notional, the mental freedom of being unchained from 'what is' allows you to have a glimmer of 'what can be'. Of course, you then have to go back in and make it happen, but even retaining some of the sense of making a fresh and creative start will make a great difference.

The reason this works is because life is a series of discontinuities: it's great moments like our first kiss, our excitement at seeing a hero or heroine, or sad events such as deaths and separations, that really draw incisive lines across the predictable trajectory of our lives. Firing yourself is one way of using this notion of discontinuity in a positive way.

But it's easy to say 'Take an afternoon off and just sit and think'. In our frenetic world most people find this rather threatening or somehow not 'productive' (see how the language of the machine and efficiency seeps into our everyday speech).

Therefore, find a friend, muse or mentor to have this conversation with.

A colleague who found himself impossibly busy and stretched in his own family business, with children from past and present relationships to manage, had the courage to fire himself for three days from his own life. He spent the time shopping, walking, talking, and drinking with a friend who helped him to re-think his priorities. At this critical stage in his life he had realized that sometimes when there is too much to do, the only strategy is to do nothing. Temporarily fire yourself from your life or work. When everything is too upfront and close, clear perspective eludes us.

RE-THINK NO. 5: NEW PEOPLE, NEW IDEAS

Hang around more

Continuing from the theme of firing ourselves, it's clear that disrupting set patterns of activity and thought can help us rekindle our creativity. So let's consider for a moment *where* we are when we get our good ideas.

For most of us it's clearly not sitting at our desk, or gazing into a computer screen. It's when we are out walking, driving, or in the shower. The ability to accelerate this process of having eureka moments is explored more in the chapter on intuition. But for now let's just think that we need to hang around in places and with people and ideas that are outside our normal patterns. Of course, it's not just being in a different place, but our attitude when we are there that can open our mind.

In your field, are you hanging out with the people who have the same views and experience that you do? It's an almost certain recipe for disaster if you are looking for the Next Big Idea, because these usually come not from the mainstream with its heavy investment in yesterday's and today's winners, but from the peripheral vision that you can access when you spend time with provocative, maverick fringe thinkers. The BBC recently organized a conference on new trends in viewing, which demanded a creative response. They were at first shocked, but later found their curiosity usefully awakened by being joined at their executive seminar by body-pierced teenagers who watched a lot of global TV through the Internet without ever bothering to tune into the UK's mainstream channels.

The Road Less Travelled

When you drive home from work, do you always take the same route? When you go to a party, do you naturally gravitate to the people you are familiar with? Why not find a new route home and stop and be curious about that interesting shop/museum/park you always pass by?

If you are of a curious bent of mind, these meetings shouldn't need to be artificially engineered. You will naturally go out of your way to find people whose thinking is a little out of the ordinary because as we all know intellectually, but forget time and again, today's fringe is tomorrow's mainstream. Listen to Nicholas Negroponte, founder of MIT's Media Lab, describe where new ideas come from:

> *'New ideas come from differences. They come from having different perspectives and juxtaposing different theories ... New concepts and big steps forward, in a very real sense, come from left field, from a mixture of people, ideas, backgrounds and cultures that normally are not mixed.'*

So find new people, outrageous ideas, and keep your mind open for as long as possible without going insane. Or allow yourself to be un-sane – that is, not trapped in your everyday sense of sanity – long enough to gain valuable ideas from people and situations you've probably unconsciously prevented yourself from experiencing.

Buy a new newspaper

Most people are familiar with the expression 'you are what you eat'. Perhaps less often considered is the notion that we are what we *read*. As with people, we gravitate towards newspapers, TV and commentary that satisfies our own fragile need to have the world rebuilt as our prejudices would like it to be. When I make the following suggestion – that we read a new newspaper every day to get out of this rut – people in the audience are usually horrified. Change my childcare arrangements? Possibly. Change my way of working? It's worth considering. Change my partner? Not out of the question. But somehow, particularly in the UK, the paper we read is sacrosanct.

In fact, varying our daily source of news intake is only one way of being more curious about what other people outside our own chosen circle are thinking.

> *When you are next going on a long journey or flight or have a day off, buy half a dozen magazines that are on the periphery of your usual preoccupations.*

For instance, you might explore architecture, design, gardening, music – remembering that so many ideas come from peripheral vision. It's amazing how often subjecting your mind to unusual influences allows you to make creative connections back to your own situation. This can even occur in mundane activities like washing the dishes, when your mind is freewheeling and able to make intuitive associations. This is what happened to glass-maker Pilkington, who observed how dishes seemed to float on the soapsuds in the sink, and made the mental leap to a method of manufacturing glass while it floats in a tank.

Dipping into unfamiliar reading material gives you at least the basic language to have a conversation with somebody in a parallel or completely different field who you will meet when you 'hang around' more. This works when you acknowledge your ignorance as well as your inflamed curiosity about the subject.

Creativity can be thought of as making unusual, but useful, connections between one field and another. Gary Hamel, a leading researcher on innovation, observed this in retailer Marks & Spencer. One of their executives made a connection between a silkscreen process used to print patterns on fabric and the need to efficiently butter bread for their huge sandwich business. A simple but imaginative re-use of technology.

Of course, we've limited ourselves if we merely think of getting news from a paper – try logging on, for instance, to the New York Times (www.nytimes.com) or specialist websites such as www.creativearchive.bbc.co.uk. Rather than spoon-feed the news to you, these sites allow you to drill down more deeply into any areas that interest you.

A more radical re-think is not to buy the papers at all.

For at least three months a year I find it very useful to have a news holiday, and to use the time I might otherwise have spent listlessly reading, say, the Personal Finance section of the Sunday paper (guaranteed to make you anxious), to read books or more in-depth analysis of the stories behind the stories. Apart from the great release from anxiety, fear and general *ennui* brought on by reading the clever but cynical output of most journalists, the British in particular, I'm sure that this keeps my mind fresher and more open. There is something very staccato in the way that we receive news flashes, sound bites, and largely repetitive *reportage.* I'm convinced this afflicts us all with some degree of attention deficit syndrome, as well as a more negative outlook on life.

Absorb yourself in something more timeless and you develop the ability to concentrate and follow through on an idea in a more sustained and absorbed way.

If this seems too extreme, try buying all the papers just one day a month and reading them cover to cover. Or buy an acceptable summary, such as *The Week*. You won't miss a lot.

Read something more challenging

I always have on the go what I call 'Lifetime Achievement' books. The achievement is all mine, if I can finish them, but it's good to have something higher to reach for. Here's my list. I suggest you make your own and get stuck in straight away – pick ones that are not for the faint-hearted and you've got the idea.

Shakespeare and the Goddess of Complete Being by Ted Hughes.

Godel, Escher, Bach: An Eternal Golden Braid by Douglas Hofstader.

A Glastonbury Romance by John Cowper Powys.

The Death of Forever by Darryl Reaney.

The Bhagavad Gita translated by Maharishi Mahesh Yogi.

Silence by John Cage.

Not only are these all great, parts of them are so rich that I continually get stuck in certain sections in a contemplative reverie, surely a desirable effect of reading something that's on the cusp of one's ability to fully comprehend.

Have to hand a good etymological dictionary (word origins – if you've been directed to the butterfly section, you've spelt it wrong) and then you can really begin to educate yourself. The same is true of a well-written magazine such as *The Spectator*. I usually have to reach for the dictionary two or three times and the diversion becomes the journey. The best-known and truest tip for improving your own vocabulary and ability to speak and write is *to read well-written material*. (Then allow yourself a bit of a holiday with a John Grisham.)

Every few years I attempt Proust's *A La Recherche du Temps Perdu*. I get myself fit by reading some lighter French stuff, have a good run up and see how far I can read before the sheer impossibility of the enterprise gets me down. Page 132 of *Swann's Way*, the first book in the series of six volumes, is my record to date, but I'm hoping to beat this sometime soon.

Proust's brother Robert commented that because of the sheer size of Marcel's output, you'd have to have a broken leg or be ill in bed for a long time to manage it. This not only makes me feel better, but also indicates that people had problems with paying attention as early as the first decades of the twentieth century.

RE-THINK NO. 6: THINGS TO BE CURIOUS ABOUT

Where you live

I'm continually amazed by how little most people know about their immediate surroundings. In a street in London a famous retailer has its headquarters opposite a large mounted statue. I tried a small experiment and asked people who had been in the building for a year or two who this was a statue of. Most had no idea, and one even replied 'What statue?'

This is how familiarity in our perceptions breeds contempt, and it means we are missing a great deal of enrichment from our own intimate environment.

The most immediate way of discovering your surroundings is to read and hear the stories that encapsulate its history. Buy an interesting guide today and become more curious about your own patch.

I'm lucky enough to live in Oxford, which has a very rich history, and for me it's the stories that really bring the city to life. For instance, when I walk past Queen's College in the High, I'm always reminded of a description of the wildness of its students, mainly of northern stock, in the nineteenth century: 'From the gentleman in the back quad at Queen's, "Good Lord, deliver us", prayed the frightened students of a near-by college when the Queen's College mob emerged each morning, hair unwashed and unkempt (even though the statutes provided for a permanent barber in the college) armed with bows, arrows, dogs, and musical instruments, all of which were forbidden by the founder.'[2]

Naturally, all of our stories are entwined with our own very personal perceptions, and I also recall well-lubricated evenings at Queen's College Smoker events where friends played in a jug band.

Or walking near to my own college, I enjoy the romantic architecture of Hawksmoor in All Souls and think of the time in the 60s when its reactionary Warden, John Sparrow, was railing against the strange desire of dons to become married. He wanted them all to enjoy breakfast at the college in order to create a manly, monastic community, and questioned: 'Why would anybody want to give up All Souls for one body?'

Whenever I walk past the Martyr's Memorial – marking the seventeenth-century burning of Bishops Cranmer, Ridley and Latimer in central Oxford – I am reminded of another story. A tourist asked a taxi driver the names of the martyrs. Perhaps wishing to receive a handsome tip and not wanting to admit ignorance, he replied that they were called 'Freeman, Hardy and Willis, sir', a well-known chain of shoe retailers in the UK.

But wherever you live, there will be older people who remember the past history, characters and anecdotes about your own patch.

---

[2] *Oxford Oddfellows and Funny Tales*, Breen and Mudannayake, Penny Publishing Ltd, London, 1977.

Be curious in seeking these stories and you will develop a greater enjoyment of your own home territory. As well as becoming a better host.

Your own story

I focused this chapter on re-thinking mundane habits, such as the newspaper you read, but this is not to exclude being curious about questions that seem too big to make a start on, such as *Who am I? Where do I come from? What's my purpose in this life?* It's easy to sneer at these questions as the preoccupations of the well-to-do with too much time on their hands. But all avenues of curiosity, including being more curious about others, will lead you to better self-understanding.

If you are lucky enough to have elderly relatives still alive, be curious and bold enough to ask for more stories about your own life, your upbringing, towns you lived in that you can't now recall, people you have forgotten.

All too often we have only the frequently repeated two or three anecdotes about our childhood. They are usually tinged with the embarrassment that only parents can inflict upon us. But if we explore further we will not only shine a fresh light on a dusty memory, but also learn family tales that we never knew.

Inevitably, some secrets will emerge. Now some of these are best not to know, but just ask yourself whether you have really taken the time to explore your own story to your satisfaction before it's too late. I remember making a journey to visit people who had known my grandfather, who died when I was three, and it was both fascinating and strangely reassuring to discover which of the family stories seemed to have been polished up and which were clearly true.

Curiosity about genealogy is one avenue but I suspect you will discover more from stories told by the living than from family trees. History is, after all, a story or series of stories.

Naming

Most of us have a poor understanding and a surprising lack of curiosity about the names of people, places and things, and the impact of these names. Have you ever wondered about why you are probably not very good at remembering people's names? One of the reasons is that we are not curious enough about the source and meaning of a person's name, which is a more powerful influence in their life than perhaps they realize. Every time a name is spoken there is a certain resonance, both for the listener and the owner. Many ancient cultures recognize this, and have elaborate and meaningful processes for naming people that we have almost completely abandoned in the Western world.

The meaning of names

'Must a name mean something?' Alice asked doubtfully. 'Of course it must,' Humpty Dumpty said with a short laugh, 'my name means the shape I am – and a good handsome shape it is, too. With a name like yours, you might be any shape, almost.'

Lewis Carroll, *Through the Looking Glass*, 1871.

Alice, by the way, means 'proud' –
and in this specific case also 'priggish'.

I say completely abandoned, but I believe that a trace remains. It's uncanny how often there is some hidden meaning in our names, which comes to resonate with our nature. For instance, my own name Nigel is from a Celtic word meaning, literally, the dark one. Superficially this doesn't make any sense as I am not particularly dark, and yet from school days onward my nature has been to appear quite lazy, and then suddenly surprise people by switching into another gear when I have a passion for something. In other words, I was often called 'the dark horse.'

Now, to be pragmatic, I don't care whether this theory is true or not, but I find it *useful.* Reflecting on my own personality has helped me to construct a life where I am able to do more of what I am passionate about.

Research the origins and meaning of your own names, family, middle and forename. You may need to read about this or simply ask relatives.

A more striking example is a late family friend, Casey. He was given the name K C, after Kadesh, the Hebrew for prayers for the dead. He changed KC to Casey as it was gloomy, but became famous in America for his lifelong efforts preventing people on death row from being executed. He was often successful and in a very real sense his life had become a prayer for the dead.

I can hear many 'yes, buts' crowding in. What about someone called Bert who also saves lives? And how will Brooklyn Beckham, named after the place where he was conceived, be influenced by this in his life? I'm not asking you to believe in a theory, but merely to expand your curiosity by talking to other people about their names (perhaps middle names that you never hear) and their own attitudes towards them. You'll be surprised by what you learn.

Naming in a work environment is also important. A friend who used to work at the UK Car Works in Longbridge described to me how depressing it was to approach his place of work clearly labelled LARGE CARS – BLOCK D. There's been a superficial re-branding of roles in organizations today, calling people 'associates' or 'partners', for instance. Except in the case of the admirable John Lewis Partnership, which has no outside shareholders and where people who work in the business literally *are* the partners and share in the company's profits, this renaming is usually just tinkering.

If the intention is to make these often mundane jobs really live up to the word, then I'm all for renaming. Though with natural English reserve I'd find it hard to be the American consultant who gave me a business card labelling his job as 'Director of Client Wow!'

If you think you have trouble describing to your children in the evening what you do for a living, then you still have it easy compared with this man. Which may, of course, make his family conversations more interesting.

The power of names

J R R Tolkien is one of the world's most famous fiction writers. He was a literature professor and something of a linguist, and this passion shines through in the resonance of the names he gives to characters and places. I can't think of any other writer who I last read decades ago, whose names I can remember so vividly. The charge contained in these names is, I'm sure, partly responsible for the success of his work.

Tolkien believed that the English should learn Icelandic, because of the richness of its sagas, and the influence of the language on Early English. I was recently thinking about Tolkien when I was in Reykjavik and at that moment looked up and saw a building with one word on it: Gimli.

To name a book, an idea, a record, a film or a product in a fresh way doesn't guarantee success, but it certainly helps. People marketing a new gizmo do have systems for arriving at a winning name – there may be millions at stake.

This is why we get a justified rush of *schadenfreude* when they come up with a real dummy, like Nissan's model for the Australian market, christened ... the Cedric. Cedric is not a fellow who is likely to be served a can of Fosters in most parts of Australia, except certain parts of Sydney. And writer Tom Peters positively fumes over the lack of imagination exhibited by Gillette, when after millions of dollars of research to produce and market their new three-blade razor (son of Mach 1 and Mach 2) they gave it the name – wait for it – the Mach 3!

Names can be a source of differentiation in a crowded market. Flicking through the *Yellow Pages* recently to find a chimney sweep,[3] I ended up hiring the one who described himself as a 'sootologist'. Of course, sometimes it's playing on associations with the name that can give you a creative edge. I expect that these Caribbean undertakers have won business with the chutzpah of their advertisement:

LAZARUS & Co
Funeral Directors
We Have Your Size!

The naming of books has always been a fertile field for re-thinking. There's a lot to be said for book titles that include their whole message in seed form:

Feel The Fear And Do It Anyway (Just do it!)

---

[3] One of my favourite T-shirt mottos, seen recently at a music festival, read 'Too Many Children, Not Enough Chimneys'.

Tough Love (Giving them what they want isn't enough)

Men Are From Mars, Women Are From Venus (Er … they're different)

On Being A Good Enough Parent (Cancel that domestic goddess seminar)

Zen and the Art of Motorcycle Maintenance (It's hard to find a more striking juxtaposition)

If the title's concise enough, perhaps there's no need to read the content. You've got the whole message, or as much of it as you're ever likely to, without reading a word. In the wonderful invented language of science fiction writer Robert Heinlein, you've *grokked* it. (Translation: understood the concept in one whole gulp.)

In fact, this makes for a great parlour game that sharpens up your creative grasp of language. Try making your own list of dreadful and brilliant names, swap with friends and you have enough material to make the dullest evening swing. Finding joy in names sharpens your observation.

In popular music my favourite group name is Half Man, Half Biscuit, and in particular their bizarre song titles, which include 'Outbreak Of Vitas Gerulitas' and 'All I Want For Christmas Is A Dukla Prague Away Kit'. I'd give a close second position to Gefilte Joe And The Fish and their surprisingly minor hit, 'A Walk On The Kosher Side'. A final wonderful book title is *The Little Book of Wrong Shui: How to Drastically Improve Your Life By Basically Moving Stuff Around – Honest.*[4]

[4] Rohan Candappa, *The Little Book of Wrong Shui: How to Drastically Improve Your Life by Basically Moving Stuff Around – Honest,* Ebury Press, 1999.

Curious about nature

Many of us are ignorant of the names of trees and plants found in the hedgerows. On one springtime walk in England I learned to recognize and name the following flowers: Lords and Ladies, Cowslip, Snakeshead Fritillary, Kings Cup, Magnolia, Plantain.

Learning the names of things adds so much richness to a simple activity like a country walk. Refresh your mind by exploring and learning the names of, for instance, flowers, plants, planets or architectural styles.

re-think | three

Intuition and eureka

When we intuit a really fresh solution, it seems that we are thinking without thinking. Intuition is an accelerated form of re-thinking where the disparate parts of a problem suddenly snap into place like the pieces of a jigsaw. The answer just *feels* right.

We're all aware of that rush of inspiration or moment of clarity when the mental fog surrounding the problem lifts. The sheer suddenness of it often takes us by surprise. A picture has come into focus, just like the moment when an image in your camera or binoculars becomes clear.

Many people have likened this process to discovering or unveiling a truth that was always there. Picasso encapsulates this when he says, '*Je ne cherche pas, je trouve.*'

How, where and when do we allow these moments of insight to occur in our own lives?

In its most concentrated form, we experience intuition as a *eureka*. Some of the most famous examples are Einstein on a tram in Zurich suddenly cognizing how our perception of time and space is affected by the relative motion of the observer; Mozart hearing the whole of a symphony in his head at one moment; Newton's moment of clarity about gravity as an apple fell on his head and, of course, Archimedes leaping from his bath and running through Syracuse crying 'Eureka!'

While it's good to understand the creative process in these individuals, too much emphasis on them leads to a distancing of you and I from the same creative process that's at work in all of us. When Einstein said that Mozart was 'only a guest on this earth' he was describing the sublime nature of his creations. But this puts him one level removed from the reality that you and I experience.

So let's demystify intuition and its role in our own creativity.

Where are you when you get your good ideas? Psychologists describe the trinity of *the bath, the bed and the bus*: activities in which we have ceased to analytically tackle a problem, and yet the apparently free-wheeling mind is still processing the pieces of the puzzle. The Chinese scholar Ouyang Hsiu said there were three situations where his writing was at its best: on the pillow, on horseback and on the toilet. And just listen to Mozart's description of the moments in which ideas were most accessible to him:

> *'When I am, as it were, completely myself, entirely alone, and of good cheer – say, travelling in a carriage, or walking after a good meal, or during the night when I cannot sleep; it is on such occasions that ideas flow best and most abundantly. Whence they come I know not; nor can I force them.'*[1]

The first part of this observation is practically useful to us: it describes the kind of preconditions and environment that we might need for the creative juices to flow. But he also acknowledges the mystery.

---

[1] Jagdish Parikh, *Intuition, the New Frontier of Management,* Blackwell Publishers Inc, 1994, page 44. Reproduced by permission, Blackwell Publishing Ltd.

Now, while we might not be an Einstein or a Mozart, we all recognize those moments of breakthrough in thinking – it could be a mini-eureka about what to say to your partner, how to give a presentation, why you should give your love to this person – and you may have sat wondering where the idea came from. But it's as if the idea springs fully formed into one's mind, while logic scurries to catch up.

> *Intuition is the sudden arrival at a solution with the logical steps hidden from our conscious mind. The idea stands up to logic, but that's not how you got there. It's thinking without thinking.*

Intuition is probably at play in most decisions we make, and dramatically illustrated in the famous breakthroughs I've just described. But look for hard research on intuition and you'll find it strangely elusive. Works by major writers about the brain – for instance Steven Rose and Thomas Pinker – hardly carry a reference to it. Ironically, many of the breakthroughs in understanding that they are describing came through sudden bursts of mental clarity. Fortunately, science is catching up: the role of emotions and even the study of consciousness have begun to be legitimate areas for research thanks to the groundbreaking thinking of neuroscientists like Antonio Damasio.

Carl Jung once remarked that it was very stupid to regard everything we cannot explain as a fraud. Naturally this does not mean that we should abandon logic in trying to understand intuition. Jung, who was largely responsible during the last century for raising our awareness of intuition, observed, *'[intuition] does not denote something contrary to reason, but something outside the province of reason.'*

It's as if in our intuitive moments we dip into a well of potential solutions, which is not available to the reasoning process alone. But it only stands up as a truthful insight if we can then work backwards and apply reason to it. For instance, had Archimedes or Einstein been wrong in their intuitive leaps, or Mozart produced poor music, we wouldn't be talking about their intuitive flash.

Our hunches, gut feelings, or moments of inspiration should be tempered with rational reflection. Here's how to balance both sides of our nature and prime the mind for more eureka moments.

The eureka cycle

Imagine you are doing a difficult crossword puzzle. Unless you are a genius at these things, after a while you will probably realize that the best strategy is to put it down, leave it and apply the old wisdom of sleeping on it. You pick it up again later in the day, perhaps the next morning, and what happens? Immediately some of the solutions that you were blind to the day before become astonishingly obvious.

Stages of creative problem solving

1 Preparation/analysis

2 Incubation/synthesis

3 Illumination/eureka

4 Execution/testing

When we explore how this happens, we can see that it's like the process of re-thinking anything in our lives. We can put this into the systematic framework in the box above. I've adopted this from the work of the great French mathematician Henri Poincaré, whose breakthroughs came in visual flashes following long periods of analysis.

The first stage is the period of analysis in our crossword example. Is it an anagram? Which sense of the word is meant here? Does this word fit? When we leave it alone to incubate (stage 2), it's clear that we have consciously forgotten the problem, but that our mind is working at synthesizing it. We may have relaxed and let it go, but this is a very fertile time for the mind to be making connections beneath the threshold of our consciousness. Hopefully, the next stage is to have the *aha* or *eureka* experience, and we test this in stage 4, when we find that our answer to the clue fits, or doesn't. (Or when working with my dyslexic wife, who decides to *make* it fit!)

Now this is the same process – albeit in a more everyday setting – as that at work when Einstein considered General Relativity. Many years of analysis preceded his flash of intuition, and the insight or eureka only made sense to him because he had a logical context to place it in.

Let's relate this to everyday problem solving.

You've been focusing hard on something in your work or on a personal problem. So when you go out for a meal after work or relax at the weekend, you completely forget about it. Or do you? Most of us have experienced getting good ideas about work when we are not at work or a relationship when we have some distance from it. Sitting on the beach, in the garden, driving the car, in the shower – all these moments when we have stood back enough from the problem to allow a clearer perception to emerge. *It may not be as dramatic as a major scientific or artistic breakthrough, but it's the same process at work.*

We can make sense of this through our understanding of the brain's two hemispheres. The left hemisphere is more associated with sequential, logical, numerate and rational activities; the right in most people is more dominant in visual, spatial, musical processing, and links more immediately to our emotional centres.

But be careful. The pop psychology view of this is to say the left side of the brain is the villain of the piece because it's merely logical, preventing the good guy in the right hemisphere from coming up with creative pictures. When you look at the model above, you'll see this is misleading. Stage 1 has a *tendency* towards analysis of the component parts of the problem and is essential so that the synthesis, or more right hemisphere activities, have something to piece together!

Looking up the answers

If you're doing a puzzle book, how often do you cheat and look at the answers at the back? What if we were able to do this in everyday life? The answer is that we can: projecting in your own mind into the future, it's amazing how often an answer just comes to us if we are only still long enough to ask for it. Try now. *Sit quietly with a problem or issue you want to solve and just think what the answer in the back of the book would be.*

The eureka stage can be described as both hemispheres of the brain functioning together. An answer that stands up to logic has been arrived at, but it didn't happen in incremental steps, such as analysis of statistics.

Intuition short circuits logic and may confound it, but it's a coming together of *both* modes of thought that yields a truly useful creative idea as opposed to a right-side-of-the-brain fantasy. Those are the dreams that are just clouds in your coffee. Real creativity means bringing something into being – or a connection between two previously unconnected strands of thought – and giving it form and structure. It's being a dreamer, but one who *does.*

Two-second intuitions

The *New York Times* science writer Malcolm Gladwell describes in his fascinating book *Blink* how we often make two-second judgements of a situation, a process very akin to what we would commonly call intuition. He strikingly describes how an expert on Greek art, when presented with what was supposed to be a *kouros*, a genuine ancient statue, made a judgement in seconds based apparently on feeling whether it was genuine. One expert had a sense of 'intuitive repulsion' based on just an initial glance. The Getty Museum have paid $10 million for this statue based on over a year's worth of scientific analysis with an electron microscope, mass spectrometry, x-ray defraction, and other analytical methods that said it was definitely genuine. Who are we to believe?

Now if someone with little knowledge of these matters – like myself – had made the intuitive judgement that it was a fake, my perception would have little or no value. When you or I come to a 'blink', or sudden judgement, it's as if *years of preparation and knowledge are compressed into that moment of insight*. This is why, in one of the most famous defamation cases, the artist James Whistler was able to declare that although his paintings took only a very short time to create, he poured the experience of a lifetime into each one.

A crossword puzzle of course has an optimum, or right answer. The important matters we deal with in life are more open-ended problems or opportunities where the search for an answer is far more fluid. For instance, we may have a 'eureka' and then test it to find that we need to do a lot more analysis for it to be a sensible solution, or we may find that we have flashes of insight during the first phase.

The important thing is to realize that this pattern of analysing, incubating and illumination seems to be hard-wired into our brains, and is the way that we think about life's bigger issues. Just being more aware of which stage we are in with a specific topic can help us to relax and receive the gifts that come from this natural cycle of brain activity. It's as if our mind *wants* to give us a solution, scanning the environment for possible answers.

Deeper levels of thinking and feeling

So far we've been looking at a sequential view of how we have good ideas. We also need to think in a vertical dimension. What are the different *levels* of thinking and being that give birth to new ideas?

In the pyramid visual you will see different levels of knowing. At the surface our rational mind; underpinning this, our emotions and intelligence.

The last level of the pyramid I've described as 'knowingness'. This is not as mysterious as it may sound. Your rational mind may take a while to catch up with your feelings, but in the words of a very pragmatic friend I asked to define intuition, 'You just know!' This is the level of

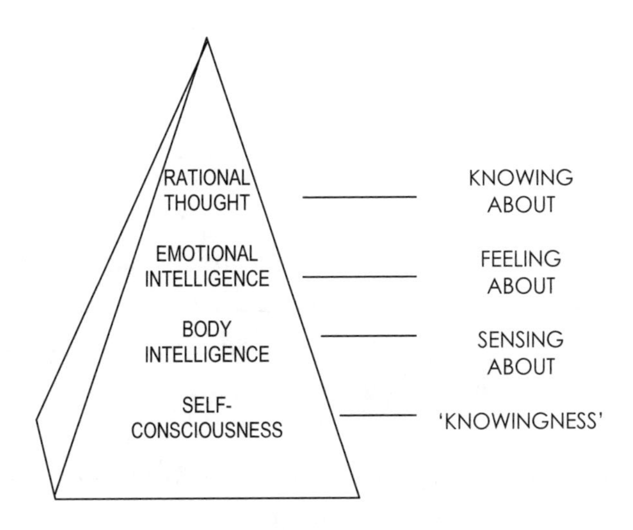

implicit rather than *explicit* knowledge – you may not be able to rationalize how or why you know, but you *just know*.

Creativity is essentially a more connected type of thinking. Too much working at the surface level of the ocean of thought and we are focusing merely on the parts. Learn to transcend these more superficial levels and we are tapping into more 'whole' thinking where these parts are re-combined in ways our divided, either/or thought processes cannot see.

Intuition is a way of diving into deeper levels of an ocean or lake. This is where more powerful ideas reside, and nowhere is this better captured than in these words of Arthur Koestler:

> *'The moment of truth, the sudden emergence of a new insight, is an act of intuition. Such intuitions give the appearance of miraculous flashes, or short-circuits of reasoning. In fact, they may be likened to an immersed chain of which only the beginning and the end are visible above the surface of consciousness. The diver vanishes at one end of the chain and comes up at the other end, guided by invisible links.'*[2]

How then do we learn to be more receptive to this, and how do we know which insights to trust and which ones to dismiss as mere flights of fancy or superstitions?

---

[2] *The Act Of Creation,* Arthur Koestler, Macmillan, 1970.

Head south for intuition?

'*Thinking* is a predominant characteristic of the structured organizations of the North. It can also be seen in Britain as more Scottish than English, and in Italy as more Piedmontese than Neapolitan. Thoughtful analytical management, then, adopts an objective approach to decision-making.

'*Feeling,* conversely, is a predominant characteristic of the personalized organizations of the South. It is more Irish than Scottish, more African than European, more humanist than rationalist.'

Intuition, The New Frontier of Management by Jagdish Parikh, Blackwell Business, 1994, p. xxii.
Reproduced by permission of Blackwell Publishing Ltd.

Let's start with what *not* to do. Don't stereotype yourself as not being an intuitive type. Despite the everyday expression, 'woman's intuition', a *feel* for what is the right course of action is available to all of us, although interestingly men prefer the more masculine language of 'gut feel' or 'hunches'. A management school professor, Jagdish Parikh, has conducted large surveys of people from many cultures and discovered that intuition is a commonly used tool for decision-making by both women and men. Interestingly, it's given greater importance by older people. Perhaps the younger MBA-trained types have yet to 'unlearn' the more academic mindset that business is a purely rational process of getting in the numbers, crunching them, and coming up with the right conclusions. Here's an observation from an unlikely source, the Austrian School of Economics:

> *'Business is an intuitive activity involving hunches and gut feeling.'*

Much of the theory about intuition comes from Carl Jung's description of a continuum with pragmatic thinking derived from the senses at one end, and intuition at the other. You can be given a score on this scale for psychological inventories like the Myers-Briggs Type Indicator (MBTI) showing your preference for these two types of problem-solving.

Now while this does demonstrate a *preference* – almost all of us are asymmetrical in having a preference for left or right hand, eye, ear, foot, etc. – I believe a health warning needs to come with these types of instruments. Once you have your results you may tend to act in a way that becomes a self-fulfilling prophecy. 'I'm a rational type, so I don't do intuition,' or 'I'm intuitive so I'm not very good at analysis.'

The learning should be to stretch, not strain, one's capacity to include some of the positive attributes of the undeveloped style.

The potential trap here, and a barrier to many attempts to successfully re-think anything, is 'either/or' thinking, a channel of thinking that is educationally reinforced by our obsession with verbal and numerate skills. Put simply, our overemphasis on book learning and analytical types of intelligence that don't value, for instance, emotional and creative intelligence.

Both/and thinking

'The test of a first-rate intelligence is the ability to hold two opposed ideas in the mind at the same time, and still retain the ability to function.'

F Scott Fitzgerald, novelist, 1896–1940.

There are deeper *levels* of intelligence that underpin all this conscious thinking. Too much of our attention is with the two-dimensional plane of either/or: the notion of *levels* of existence allows us to see a solution, as it were, in three dimensions. In other words, from many different angles. I call this 'both/and' thinking – *both* able to see the more observable levels of a problem *and* the less obvious aspects that are invisible to this mode of thought. The levels of feeling, and also what has been called 'body intelligence'.

It's not accidental that we use expressions like 'gut' feel when we can't explain logically why we know something. The body itself has its own 'brains'. Think of the thousands of decisions being made for us every second by our digestive systems. Scientists call this gut motility, increasingly realizing that the 'mind has escaped from the brain': the whole of our nervous system is involved in feeding messages that may eventually appear as conscious thought in the higher thinking centres in the cortex of our brains.

One of the world's most successful financiers, George Soros, talks of having a pain in his back that alerts him to the dangers in a particular investment decision. Remember, this is *both/and*: it doesn't mean he abandons his rational knowledge of the stock market in making decisions. Rather, that he's also informed by deeper levels of his intelligence. In this case, intuition is literally 'embodied' in the nervous system.

So how do you listen to the role your emotions play? The simple answer is to *ask*. You need to be relaxed and, ideally, in a quiet place to have this conversation with yourself, closer to the level of knowingness.

Intuition is a bodily as well as mental experience, so a simple exercise is to turn and face each of the four directions of the compass, assessing in turn the state of your Mind, Body, Emotions, and

Spirit when you are considering a specific situation or problem. Write down or sketch without censorship what comes to you.

You can also use this to address bigger questions in life, such as:

How do you feel as you get ready for work?

What is your general level of health?

The latter question has been found by medical doctors to be a surprisingly accurate diagnostic tool. If you can be still enough to get in touch with a level of 'just knowing', it's surprising how your ability to decide the right course of action improves.

It takes practice and time to do this, just like learning or re-learning any particular skill. Ideas often come to us in silence, and making a daily practice of sitting quietly and holding, but not straining on, a particular problem in your mind and checking in with your feelings and body inevitably trains you to 'feel' your way to a better solution. When I say that you are contacting a level of your mind at which you just 'know', this has been understood in some philosophies for thousands of years. This level of the mind is known in India as *ritam* – the level that only upholds truth. So when Einstein *knew* that his theories were right, he wasn't being arrogant, but expressing the certainty that comes from tapping into the level of knowingness.

Letting go of anxiety and fear is the first step. Don't worry, you've always got your rational gatekeeper to check that your insights make sense. The trick is to switch it off for a while. Tell it to get out a bit more often and try something new.

Unwritten rules

'There's a basic rule that runs through all kinds of music, a kind of unwritten rule. I don't know what it is. But I've got it.'

Ron Wood, guitarist with the Rolling Stones

RE-THINK NO. 7: ACCELERATING EUREKAS

Let's suppose you have a task that requires a degree of creative thinking to complete in, say, a week's time. It might be an article you are writing, a presentation to colleagues, a personal conversation you are really uncertain about, or an interview. For simplicity's sake, let's assume this occurs on a Friday and you are only able to deal with it in the few days prior.

People differ in their planning habits, but many leave the preparation until the Thursday. Or if brinkmanship is your speciality – until Friday morning! A good idea, like a good wine, needs time to be set aside and to mature in its own way. Applying the four-stage model of analysis, incubation, eureka and execution, the ideal is to start on the Monday, leave the problem aside until the Wednesday, and then try to formulate your ideas more fully. Why does this yield ideas that are so much better?

It's because once you have fed all the data into your mind – we'll look at methods for this shortly – you are incubating and synthesizing even while you are consciously dealing with other matters. Occasionally you may even come up with small eurekas along the way. This means that when you sit down on the Wednesday night to put your ideas together,

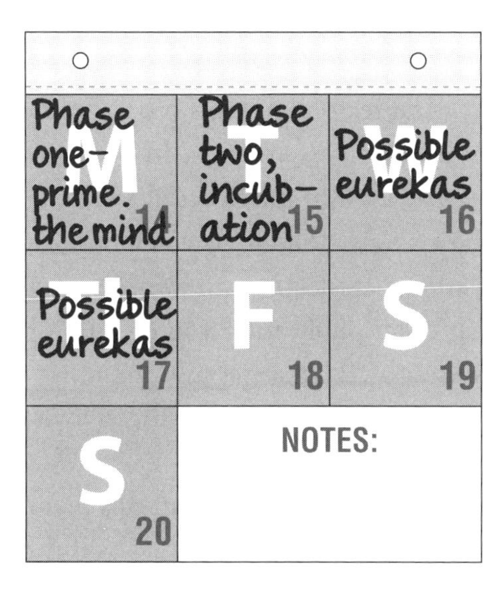

there will be a degree of effortlessness and a feeling that the ideas flow more easily. Often you are just capturing the ideas that have arisen to the conscious surface of your mind while you've been occupied with other activities.

Making a 'brainstorm' work

You may have tried to introduce a brainstorming session either at home or at work, only to experience a deep and prolonged silence when you announce the word. It's not because people don't want to be creative, but good ideas take time to mature and grow.

A magically more effective method is to talk to everybody individually a few days before about the topic you want them to be creative about. Either face to face or on the phone. In the intervening period they will have incubated the idea and possibly even had some eurekas. Even better if you ask them to bring a 'prototype' of an idea or solution rather than a blank sheet of paper to the meeting. The difference is miraculous.

There's a very practical reason why this process of saturating yourself in the topic early, and then leaving it aside, produces better ideas. It's the concept of *mental set*. You might recall from the first chapter the example of buying a new car. Suddenly you look around the roads and selectively notice similar models to your own. Or a new word or expression. It seems that every publication you pick up or TV programme you tune into is using it. This is because the mind is unconsciously scanning your environment for 'matches' for its own preoccupations.

Put into a problem-solving context, this means that if you have fed in the elements of the problem *earlier*, then it's as if the intuitive nature of the mind is looking for solutions all around you. Researchers talk about the 'library angel' – that inexplicable force that means you come across a book or an article that has just fallen open and is relevant to your search. As far as I'm aware there isn't yet an equivalent name for this when using the Internet, but one of its great contributions to thinking laterally is the ability to chase links through only tangentially connected sites.

This needn't be explained by any magical or mystical notion. It is just that the brain is hard-wired to find solutions once you have set it in the right direction. How often do you come across an article or a person who is relevant to what you have been thinking about because that's in the forefront of your mind? We know that fortune favours the prepared mind – here's how to apply this principle in everyday life.

If you're tackling a topic that needs fresh study, the best approach is to drown yourself in it for an hour or two without consciously searching for solutions.

If you've learned a technique for creative note taking, such as Tony Buzan's mind mapping, it's very useful at this stage as a way of just dumping your thoughts – like pieces of the jigsaw – on the page. It's like giving a request to your brain to start thinking about it.

Or, draw it! Ignore the 'yes, but' that says 'I cannot draw'. What I mean here is to throw the elements of the problem on a page so they are visual. Anyone can be visual without having drawing ability. It's not accidental that much of the language of intuition and creativity is ***visual***: we talk about *vision, illumination, enlightenment, seeing* a fresh solution, adopting a new *viewpoint*, or experiencing a different *perspective*. We even *draw* conclusions!

Rehearsing your ideas

An academic who lectures in economics says that if he is working on a new presentation he tries it out first on his 86-year-old mother who knows almost nothing about economics. But, being his mother, she can intuit whether he is talking nonsense or not, and in the very act of articulating the ideas, he becomes clearer about what he does and doesn't know. This is the stage of the creative process to accept and not worry unduly about the gaps in your knowledge, or the great gulf between your thinking and the solution you know you need to arrive at.

Try explaining something complex that you are working on to your children, your cat, or even a mirror. You'll certainly become clear about what you're clear about – and what you need to think further about.

A third way of starting the ball rolling early on is to talk about the idea with someone else. This acts as a mirror to your own inner workings. Often we only know what we're thinking when we hear ourselves say something!

Of course, by putting the creative problem-solving process into the pattern of a week, I am vastly oversimplifying. Sometimes we might incubate about, for instance, what's wrong in a relationship for years before that moment of clarity comes. And again, this is not a simply linear process that means that after stage 1, stage 2 must follow. There are cycles of the whole model within each phase.

So although you cannot timetable and legislate for the creative flash, you can set up some of the preconditions to make it more likely to occur. Remember Mozart's observation about his ideas, 'whence and how they come I know not; nor can I force them.'

But the one thing we can be sure of is that intuition will come to us in the gap between two thoughts, between one activity and the next, idle moments in what for most of us is an over-scheduled life, and in the gaps between sleeping and wakefulness. How to have more of those unguarded moments is the subject of our next re-think.

RE-THINK NO. 8: MIND THE GAP

Some London Underground stations have the inscription 'Mind the gap' at points where the track curls and the platform doesn't quite reach the train. A college friend of mine, sat at Bank Tube Station in an inebriated state, thought this was a message from the gods, and sat there for two hours trying to decipher what it meant. Actually, this phrase *is* quite profound when we consider how intuitive flashes come to us through the gaps in our activity, breaks in the linear tracks our minds are forced to run on. We are in a world so driven by *doing* at the expense of *being* that we usually forget the wise advice to do nothing when we can't work out what to do. To insert a useful *gap* in our thinking in which our mind can throw up the answer we are searching for.

Gaps between sleeping and waking

During a 24-hour cycle, we move between three main states of consciousness, which are both subjectively and physiologically different – sleeping, waking and dreaming. Of course, sometimes these states are not so distinct, as we may be dozing when we are meant to be reading an important document, or wide-awake thinking about our tax return in the dead hours of night.

It's long been observed that the gaps or junction points when we make a transition between two states – called the hypnagogic state – is when the veil that our busy mind draws across our inner self parts for a while to allow us a glimpse of new mental landscapes. Writer and researcher Arthur Koestler spent a lifetime thinking about the process of human creativity, and describes the state like this:

> *'The most fertile region seems to be the marshy shore, the borderline between sleep and full awakening – where the matrices of disciplined thought are already operating, but are not yet sufficiently hardened to disrupt the dreamlike fluidity of imagination.'*[3]

It's not accidental that in a creative state we talk about ideas *flowing*. Contrast this with the rigid and routine patterns of thought that usually preoccupy us. Charles Dodgson, aka Lewis Carroll, was very aware of this state and even devised a simple machine called the Nictograph, which enabled him to write down ideas in the gaps between sleeping, waking, dreaming and waking again without fully bringing himself out of sleep. For you and I, the tool just needs to be a pen and paper or, if you are sleeping alone, a dictating machine.

---

[3] Margaret Boden, *The Creative Mind*, Cardinal Book, 1990.

Gaps in your journey

It's clear that we've lost both the time and the motivation for taking walks where the journey is more important than the destination. We are hurrying to the station, to the bank, to pick up the kids from school, and often oblivious to our surroundings. The destination is everything, the journey just dead time.

Instead of just A to B, try adopting position C – noticing and taking in all the richness that's available to you on your journey. If you're driving, have the most stimulating music or ideas on a CD or the radio. If you are walking, take time to stop and explore signs, nature and individuals to have a chance conversation with. Enjoy the journey.

If you want to catch some of your best ideas, this simple advice is all you need. But beware of self-delusion. How often do we wake up after a dream and kid ourselves that we will remember it in the morning, and rarely do? It's possible to fool yourself for a whole lifetime along these lines. Have a pad and paper available – if necessary use a small booklight if you don't want to interrupt the sleep of others.

Taking a ramble

Writers like J R R Tolkien and C S Lewis were well known for sitting in the Eagle and Child pub in Oxford in their informal club, the Inklings, reading and discussing their stories over a few pints of warm English beer. What's less known about them is the energetic walks they took through the countryside. They were not the first to use the walk, or ramble, as a source of inspiration: Beethoven would stride around the city of Vienna in all weathers, dreaming up his symphonies as he strode, ignoring all who greeted him.

A good walk can bring you many creative advantages. A friend and I sometimes just set out for a morning, without a distinct plan as to where we are going to end up. With him I feel a little like Dr Watson with Sherlock Holmes because he observes people, signage and architectural details in ways that completely escape me until pointed out. The whole walk then becomes a genuine journey of discovery where we stop at certain points and perhaps continue a serious discussion. But sometimes the distractions *are* the discussion: a chance meeting, overhearing a snatch of conversation, visiting a building that wasn't open before.

On these journeys, chance conversations and encounters are welcome and our preferences are for choosing the road less travelled – a lane we hadn't been down before, a coffee shop or library not yet visited. At times like this the mind dodges in and out of daily preoccupations. Treat the creative process with the patience of a fisher, and fresh catches will break the surface of your mind. You won't be able to predict when they will happen, but almost inevitably they will.

In fact, although I am describing a ramble through the endlessly interesting streets of Oxford, it's possible to enjoy the value of a great outing anywhere. The provocatively entitled *Bollocks To Alton Towers* is a wonderful guide to finding original destinations even in some of the most urban parts of England. Alton Towers, a famous UK theme park, is here used as a metaphor for the obvious destination where everything is laid on and structured for you, and you don't have to use your imagination. By creating your own different journey you find yourself more open to ideas and impressions you weren't prepared for. The ones that come out of peripheral, left-field vision.

I'll leave you with this thought from an organization that encourages people to get out more and re-connect with the world, the Walking Society:

> *'In human history our culture is the first where our lives are not shaped by nature but by images of mass media. We spend more time watching nature TV shows than experiencing the real thing, and more evenings watching TV sex than touching another human body. Contact Earth soon.'*[4]

RE-THINK NO. 9: IDLENESS AND THE ENVIRONMENT FOR INTUITION

[4] *Resurgence Magazine*, November/December 2004, No. 227, page 35.

Studied idleness

There is an unhealthy prejudice against idleness. Study the speeches of British Politican, Gordon Brown, and you will see an obsession with the philosophy that 'getting people back to work' is the solution to all of our social and economic ills. But the creative mind is so often trapped by dull routine and the sheer exhaustion of the workaday week that we need to stage a revolt against the unholy trinity of doing, hurrying and achieving. This isn't just a modern phenomenon. Artists and creative types have often been perceived as slackers and a great danger to the hard-working merchant classes, which most of us now are. In 1885, in his book *An Apology For Idlers*, Robert Louis Stevenson said idleness '... does not consist in doing nothing, but in doing a great deal not recognized in the dogmatic formularies of the ruling class.'

Today we could say that by the ruling class we mean the prevailing *idea* in our society of seeing the work ethic as our salvation. In fact, work has become the opium of the masses. I'm not advocating using the other kind of opium, but it certainly helped Samuel Taylor Coleridge in writing the wonderful fragment *Kubla Khan.* The rest of the poem was forgotten after an interruption, a parcel delivery by a man from Porlock – surely the most reviled anonymous person in history.

If we need periods of unfocused idling, staring at the scenery, or just doing nothing in order to create the gap for our intuitive mind to fill with ideas and solutions, we have to find ways of keeping the man from Porlock from our door.

Consider this. You are a copywriter in an advertising agency and you've just been given your biggest creative assignment – to write a campaign for Heineken beer. As the days go by there is nothing on your typewriter (this was the 1980s), and your mind is either whirling or a complete blank. So what do you do? The writer in question, Terry Lovelock, left a message on his door:

> *'Gone to Marrakech. Back soon.'*

He had taken the notion of idleness to an extreme, got on to a plane to Morocco, and booked into the Hotel Mamounia. You can imagine that with the deadline fast approaching, his status in the business had sunk below zero. But in the middle of the night, he half woke to scrawl on his bedside table:

Refreshes the parts other beers do not reach

He then went back to sleep. From this one line – which poets call *une ligne donnée* – he developed one of the most successful and enduring campaigns of all time.[5]

Strangely, in appearing to do nothing, we can accomplish a great deal. This is what I mean by studied idleness. You are probably still mulling over your problem or obsession, but in a rested state so that the whole solution can surface and bypass the busy mind.

Find ways to stand back from the problem you are re-thinking – even be bold enough to take a siesta.

The nap has almost vanished from our frenetic world, and yet it's a state in which much creative work can be done. You may think that Proust was extreme in taking to his bed for 14 years to write – though doesn't that sound sublime? – but at least he created one of the greatest works of twentieth-century literature. Here's someone who was not nearly as preoccupied as you or I:

'You must sleep sometime between lunch and dinner, and no halfway measures. Take off your clothes and get into bed. That's what I always do. Don't think you'll be doing less work because

---

[5] Peter Mayle, *Thirsty Work. Ten years of Heineken Advertising.* Macmillan, 1983.

you sleep during the day. That's a foolish notion held by people who have no imagination. You will be able to accomplish more.'

This of course is Winston Churchill speaking. It's terrible that such idle downtime has almost been criminalized today. City traders feel it is a lesser crime to snort and drink to keep themselves *moving* rather than just switching off in a Churchillian fashion. When I look at people in organizations I visit at three or four o'clock in the afternoon, it is clear that many of them are exhausted, but feel the need to keep pushing on however counter-productive this is.

In Brazil's Semco this has been acknowledged by investing $30,000 (an organization shows its true values by how it spends its money) on an employee's idea of a 'Siesta Garden' of hammocks, where people can take a nap when necessary. Most importantly, there is no macho judgement that it's a sign of weakness to do so.

The environment for intuition

Given that most people say they have their good ideas either standing back from the problem or not in a work environment, I often challenge them by saying, 'Then what are you doing here in a conference room?' I'm only half joking because too often creativity is attempted in seminar rooms with two metres of table between you and the next person and airport hotels where you can't open the windows and breathe! You could say that the source of all good ideas is a bit like broadband: in theory it's there all the time and accessible to anyone with the right equipment, but in reality there are many situations where you find reception patchy or non-existent.

Writer Bill Nicholson, famous for his screenplays for *Shadowlands* and *Gladiator*, and also an award-winning children's writer, finds that he has to have a particular kind of country landscape in front of him to create at his best. He told me that ideally he likes to see lots of sky and an extensive view.

'It helps big thoughts to have a big landscape – on a clear day I can see for miles, and it's like climbing over a barrier and discovering a new-found country. It's very exciting.'

He also believes that the creative process is aided by walking on open ground. If his eyes can see far, his mind can reach out. 'On a walk, I let my brain idle. It allows slower brain waves where connections happen. I need a semi-dreamlike state to have a new idea, otherwise it's all organized by the processing brain.'

I have a particular view, looking across a wooded river valley in Gloucestershire, where I feel most relaxed and can best generate fresh thought. As I'm often not in this place I came up with the idea of taking a picture or painting of this view to other places where I write. It's not quite the same thing, but some of the memory remains with me.

Find some way to take an image of your creative spot with you when you travel.

What are the conditions that you need to think clearly, to relax and allow your intuition to flow? To inventor Denys Fisher the answer was clear. He needed three things: Beethoven played extremely loud, Irish whiskey, and the smell of rotting apples – when he was young he'd enjoyed idling in an orchard and had many of his youthful ideas and dreams there. A friend who was coaching him supplied Fisher with this dream environment, albeit in the attic of his house in Bradford, Yorkshire. He discussed the idea that Fisher was working on. The young inventor then disappeared to the attic retreat, having his meals brought to him for three days. When he came down to discuss the idea further, it was already well formulated and a name given to it. The name was 'Spirograph'. This product and its many derivatives became an international best-selling toy and artistic device.[6]

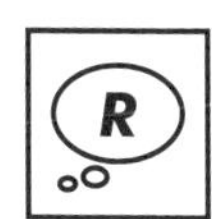

I'm not saying that Fisher wouldn't have had this idea otherwise, but it does make sense to load the dice in your favour by creating the right conditions. So where do you need to be? What props, if any, do you need? And how are you going to be ruthless in keeping the man from Porlock from your door?

I have had some of my most creative meetings with clients in unusual places, such as the top of the Arc de Triomphe, walking across the Scottish moors, at a ski restaurant in the French Alps. Given my medically certified allergy to twenty-first century offices, this has suited me just fine, but it's also worked for my clients. It's strange that even people who run a multi-billion-pound corporation feel that they are skiving or playing hooky. Afterwards they nearly always say, 'This was great, and I feel we have made a breakthrough in thinking. But I wasn't sure I'd be allowed to do it …'

Give yourself permission to be in your right mind. It works.

---

[6] Related to the author by coach and mentor Bill Driscoll.

re-think four

Paying attention

'You're not paying attention' is a criticism we all know, from school days to marriage. But we are. We're just paying attention to something more interesting than what's right in front of us, particularly the thing we feel duty bound to whip our wandering mind back to.

Who is that attractive person walking past the window? What is that music you can half hear through your neighbour's wall? The truth is that the mind goes walkabout for most of us, especially when a period of sustained attention seems necessary. Try focusing on this strange piece of poetry: *Un petit, d'un petit / S'étonne aux Halles / Un petit d'un petit / Ah! degrés te fallent*[1]

Does it seem vaguely familiar? Do you know it? You almost certainly do, but it depends what channel of attention you're using. You probably won't get it if you're (a) just saying it to yourself, or paradoxically (b) if you know French well! This is where Open-Page thinking and curiosity come into play. Once you've said it *aloud* it will come to you or, more likely, the person you're saying it to. (Answer at bottom of page.)[2]

---

[1] *Mots d'Heures: Gousses, Rames*, Luis d'Antin van Rooten, Penguin, 1967. Reproduced by permission of Penguin Group (USA) Inc.

[2] Humpty Dumpty sat on a wall, Humpty Dumpty had a great fall.

So you *did* know it! So what? Solutions to problems often come to us when we learn to use alternative ways of paying attention, when we 'play' with an idea and when our attention isn't purely passive.

Here's the good news: paying attention is not synonymous with mindless concentration, or trying hard to hold a fixed idea in our minds.

Look at your hand. Do it for, say, half a minute. What do you notice? Almost certainly your focus shifts and what you see changes.

It's almost impossible – and usually undesirable – to hold a fixed picture in your mind. We may beat ourselves up for this, saying, 'I'm no good at concentrating.'

In fact when we are trying to pay attention to a talk or a book and we find our mind has drifted off we are experiencing being 'otherwise attracted'.[3] This is the name that Harvard psychologist Ellen Langer gives to this state. The mind is always searching for whatever is most interesting and stimulating. This in/out, on/off nature of attention is a tendency we can use to good effect if we can involve or entertain the mind rather than control or corral it.

However, an understanding of creative distraction shouldn't be used as an excuse for sloth. When the full power of our attention is on someone or something, the effect is immense. There's an old saying that nothing great was achieved except by a monomaniac with a mission.

Often, it's not so much our inability to pay attention that's the problem, as *our ability to find something worthwhile to put it on.* When we find something worthy of our attention – whether it's gardening,

---

[3] Ellen J Langer, *The Power of Mindful Learning,* DaCapo Press, 1998.

fascinating work, or the chance to bring great benefit – we can become completely absorbed, even joyful in the task.

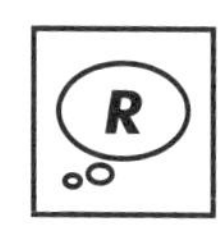

So what are those projects in your life you know will absorb your attention? Choose one and take the first small symbolic step – it may be a phone call or an email. Then do one small extra thing. Just notice on a daily basis what draws your attention in and what doesn't engage it.

Then, when you're presented with opportunities to choose between one path and another, you know which to choose.

In one of Langer's experiments on 'mindful learning', three groups of students were asked to pay attention to coloured objects on a computer screen. One group was just given the instruction to 'pay attention', another to trace the outline of the object on the screen, and the last, more mindful group were told to think in different ways about each shape and to notice different things about them.

Not surprisingly the group she calls 'mindful' out-performed the other two groups, but just as significantly, said that the task required *less* effort and was less frustrating. Langer argues that memory is the most meaningful measure of attention.

This is just one of many similar experiments demonstrating that:

'The most effective way to increase our ability to pay attention is to look for the novelty within a stimulus situation, whether it is a story, a map, or a painting.'[4]

So we *can* successfully re-think our ability to pay attention. This research is concerned with the implications for learning, but it's a lesson we can

---

4 Ibid.

apply to our personal and working lives. *Increasing novelty* and being *more active* in the way we deal with information, ideas and others is within our own control. We've already looked at novelty – ways in which we can subject our mind to new people, beliefs, fantasies and heroes – so here we'll focus on making the mind more *active* to improve our power of attention.

A more active mind

The active couch potato

There's far too much passivity in the way we take in information from books we read, TV programmes and films we see. Occasionally a great book will engage us intellectually and emotionally, but all too often the couch potato mentality stretches further than the experience of watching television. Too much hyperactive reality TV makes us feel unreal and somehow dislocated from ourselves, so here are some constructive ways in which we can nudge ourselves to become more active and involved with themes that have the potential to fascinate us.

Why not create or act out your own TV programme?

A popular series on UK television is *Back To The Floor*, where a senior executive is filmed spending a week doing a frontline job, perhaps driving a forklift truck, working in a restaurant, or answering the phone in a call centre. With a handheld video camera this is easily possible for most people to do, even at home, in a small business, school or hospital, and the effect on morale of improvements in working conditions can be a great breakthrough.

Similarly, why not adopt the philosophy of the ubiquitous makeover programmes. I particularly like the notion of *Faking It,* where a beginner in, say, surfing, horse-riding or ballroom dancing has a month to see if they can be believed to be an expert. Most give at least a good impression of being one. Don't take it too literally as if you have a full-time job – one month is probably too ambitious. You'll be amazed at how fast you can accelerate your skills. It makes you pay attention.

If you're a music lover, or were one, a fabulous evening can be had by doing your own version of the radio programme Desert Island Discs.

This is where celebrities choose eight pieces of music that were landmarks in their lives. You can do this with four or five people if you restrict everyone to three or four choices. Not only is it fascinating to hear other people's significant music, but also the conversations that follow are often more revealing than the usual dinner party variety.

Re-think music clubs – where you just take it in turns to play a piece of music and then enthuse about why you love it – could be a wonderful alternative to book clubs! If you'd like a list of different variations on music evenings, email me at nigel@nigelbarlow.com because this is a re-think I'm championing at the moment. Our ears have become less refined, blunted by the preponderance of visual media. Helping people to really listen again is the deeper motivation behind my interest in this topic.

Writing vs reading

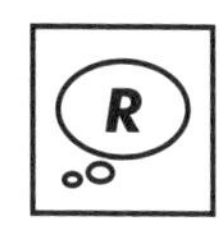

The great sage Paramahansa Yogananda said that if we read for half an hour, we should write for two hours. Keeping a journal for your eyes only is one way to help you pay attention. You can do this by writing down interesting quotations and your own thoughts or random associations with what you've just read. Or you can adopt the simple strategy advocated by Julia Cameron, author of The Artist's Way,[5] *writing what she calls the Morning Pages. This*

---

[5] Julia Cameron, *The Artist's Way: A Course in Discovering and Recovering Your Creative Self*, Pan, 1997.

means getting up and writing down without pre-thought or censorship whatever is on your mind. There are no other instructions. It's particularly valuable at difficult, stressful times in one's life.

I've introduced this idea to a number of people I've been coaching in creativity, and invariably they report that it was difficult at first, but once it became a reflex they were amazed at what emerged and its therapeutic value. 'Seeing my own preoccupations in a mirror' was how a normally ultra-rational company director described it.

Active learning

How much do schools and universities teach learners to be more active in the way they take in information? In my experience, very little – I spent several years teaching teachers ways of improving memory and understanding and found that all too often *they* were the problem. Learning methods tends to mean library skills or Internet research skills, not how to use your brain more effectively. When teachers adopt methods like Tony Buzan's colourful and visual Mind Maps as an aid to learning, they usually reduce these to black and white and linear 'spidergrams'. Learning how to learn makes an extraordinary difference to most students' abilities – it's time we appointed Buzan, or someone like him, to head up a new government department called Active Learning.

Better than dinner parties

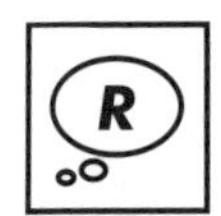

You can also introduce the idea of more active thinking into social settings. People are given a number of provocative and inspiring quotations, poems or thoughts from famous and not-so-famous people, and at dinner they take it in turns to describe which of these speak to or touch them, and why. In my experience, no po-faced intellectual conversation follows, but a great opportunity to explore more stimulating topics. Also, the chance to delve more deeply into the minds and beliefs of others.

The version I prefer is for people to come with their own two or three items to throw into the conversation. These could be quotations, music, pictures or artefacts they find meaningful, insightful, hilarious, or just beautiful. In fact, I find that having a theme to the evening works even better. Themes that have worked particularly well include beauty, authenticity, and passion. Invent your own! No one gets bored or has trouble with paying attention.

Paying attention to your day

I'm amazed how often people seem to be more interested in filming reality than experiencing it. The best camera we have, faulty though it is, is our own memory and imagination because it's so amazingly flexible – and spiced by imagination.

A family game we often play at the end of the day in order to remember a special time, weekend or holiday is to take it in turns to tell the story of the day, which we call *Where We's Bin And What We's Did*. You can do this with an adult or a child. What's wonderful is that you give your attention to the day in a very interactive way, and it can also be very revealing to discover the different ways in which you both perceived it. It creates a richer, more living archive than any video footage.

Teach it

There's no better way of being active with information than teaching it to others. Teaching is such a natural impulse that when our children learn anything new, their first reaction is to pass on the idea to another: you, their siblings, or even their favourite doll.

So if you want to both understand and remember something, adopt the same strategy. If you've ever done any teaching, you'll be aware of that 'aha' sensation that comes with trying to explain a point: halfway through explaining it you realize what it means for the first time! Or perhaps a deeper level of understanding is revealed to you. Teaching is a two-way street, and we're likely to learn as least as much as we impart.

So teach your children, your partner, your relatives about your passions and interests. To keep our attention alive, we should all be teachers.

One woman I was coaching was training as a beauty consultant, but was afraid of speaking to others in groups, a skill she would need in selling her services. Unknown to her I booked a talk for her at a local health centre six weeks ahead. For her, this was a stretch not a strain, which is an important distinction.

After her initial gut response – 'You bastard, Nigel!' – we worked on it and she acquitted herself better than she or I or her audience had expected.

Paying attention to other people – remembering names and faces

A common example of how our attention is distracted is in our inability to recall someone's name. We know that we've met them before and are frantically scrabbling in the dusty regions of our mind for their name. We may even avert our gaze and ignore them to avoid the embarrassment.

I want to describe how we can re-think and improve this ability greatly, not as a party trick or even just because it is a useful social skill – it undoubtedly is – but because it's such a striking example of how we don't pay attention.

It is said in England that when you are introduced to someone new, you don't need to have washed your face, but you do need a clean pair of shoes, because there is a tendency to avoid eye contact, gaze down and mumble your own name.

Try paying attention. People's faces are truly fascinating and almost completely unique, although we may start observing that they come in families: the pale, moon-shaped, the hawk-nosed and angular, and so on. Of course it's easy to say 'pay attention'. If we're nervous, we don't even relax enough to take in the name, and we may already be on to the first words we want to say to this person. No wonder we can't recall their name five minutes later. It's hard to *re*member what you never 'membered' in the first place.

This is an everyday instance of when to slow down the way you absorb information into your perceptual grid. Think for a minute: is a person's name important to *them*? Of course it is. Hear your own name or a similar one spoken across a crowded room and just see how immediately your mind homes in on that signal, screening out all the other background noise. We should pay attention to people's names. If we don't get it the first time, ask. If it still isn't clear, ask again.

This actually shows greater valuing of the person's individuality than filing them in your brain as Sally? Rosie? Lily? for the rest of the evening.

The scheme below takes you through the whole process of meeting and recalling a person's name. Learn it and use it – it works – but also just watch how your attention fluctuates or focuses at each stage. Also be aware, when you do use it in practice, of how *actively* processing information enhances both your attention and memory.

Names and faces – the basics

1 *Look.* Take your time to really observe the person you are meeting. Recall Sherlock Holmes' words to Dr Watson: 'You see, but you do not observe.'

2 *Question.* If you didn't get the person's name, ask them. And then ask them again. In some cases, it's also useful to start a small discussion about the name. For instance, if it's unusual, how is it spelled? What's its origin? Naturally, use this with care – if the person's name is Les Smith, I think they'll guess you are playing mind games when you say, 'Oh, how fascinating. Are you related to *Bill* Smith?' If for instance his name is 'Abramovic', the conversation might take a more interesting turn. Here you'll see the connection between attention and memory. Visualizing, exploring and playing with a concept means memory is also more likely.

3 *Re-use.* Repetition is a necessary but not sufficient requirement for recall. It helps! Use the name on introduction and perhaps two or three times during the evening, and you're beginning to groove the information into your brain.

4 *Silent review.* This, for me, is most critical: information rehearsed at more relaxed levels of the mind has a tendency to stick. There's more signal and less noise. So if it's important to remember peoples' names, I might review them several times in my head – ideally while looking at a person to make a connection, but it could be while fetching a drink. The other benefit of doing this silently is that there is no limit to the amount of times you can review the name in your own head. Some people become socially annoying because they *over-use* your name – 'Yes, Nigel. No, Nigel. You really are a fascinating person, Nigel.' Ouch.

5 *Say goodbye with the name.* Memory research shows that the first things we attend to (primacy) are recalled, as well as the last

(recency). So, if your last impression is that of recalling the name, you have a greater chance of it sticking in your memory.

But …

There's usually a great 'yes, but'. that emerges at this stage. It's often the *speed* with which you are introduced to a room of people that makes it hard to put a lot of the above into practice.

Let's address this directly.

You walk into the room and the eager host or hostess, probably two drinks ahead of you, introduces their group of friends on autopilot. 'Nigel, this is Dave, Jenny, Maya, Josh, Madeleine …' Someone may say at this time, 'I'm sure you'll forget all of that!'

Although well intentioned, this is very rude. It's tantamount to saying, 'I'd like you to meet Bob, Blob, Blobby, Whatshisname and Whoever.' Again, the technique is to *slow down the rate at which information comes to you so that you can give it full attention.*

It's actually more polite to really exchange a few words with each person in the group, and make sure they have your name and you have theirs, as well as exchanging any other social niceties, before moving on to the next one. You will have to resist the hovering presence of the hyped-up host in the background, but it can be easily done.

The next 'yes, but' is usually about the sheer volume of names. Generally, the brain is pretty good at remembering small chunks of information, about seven being the average. (Though not the norm for a trained mind.) So, for instance, if you forget your shopping list, you can probably remember about seven items, and if you're introduced to 20 or 30 people, it's regarded as doing well to remember up to seven.

If we pay attention to the way our brain processes information, we can use this ability to 'chunk' data to our benefit. So, for instance, I would usually try to have got to the silent review stage in my mind with perhaps four or five names before moving on to absorbing others. Although this sounds more rigid than the way I do it, you might decide you are going to get half a dozen names right before the coffee break, and then make sure that you get a certain amount more before lunch, and so on. Try to absorb too much, too quickly, and you're in danger of losing the lot.

The important thing at this stage is to make mistakes. People will allow you that latitude at the first meeting, but won't enjoy it too much if they're still Mr Blobby to you at your third rendezvous.

For longer-term memory, use your powers of attentive observation. If you're going to meet these people again, and it's important, a list of names is no use to you because you can't match them all with a face. Therefore, a simple sketch in your diary of someone's name and key characteristic – e.g. white-haired, black eyes, golf fanatic/Ranjit Singh – will usually do the trick.

If they were sitting in a room, putting your cryptic personal description on paper to map out where they were sitting or standing helps you to tap your visual memory. Look this up before meeting them again and you will 'get' most people. In doing this we are following the memory advice of the Greek poet Simonides, who used this kind of visual reconstruction to recall where people were sitting in a banquet hall when the roof collapsed.[6] World memory champion Andy Bell uses a similar method to remember the precise order of cards in numerous decks, mentally placing them on a city route he has really paid attention to and internalized.

---

[6] This is the origin of our everyday use of the word 'topic', taken from *topos*, the Greek for place.

Of course, stage performers use these methods and in certain situations more elaborate ones for making a connection between something quirky about the name and the physiology of the person. *Nearly everybody I speak to has the mindset – based on almost zero information – that you need these more complex techniques for recall.* You don't. For everyday purposes, the basic method above will work well enough, and is worth practising for the insight it gives us about how we can practise our powers of observation, *and* re-think our capacity to do something we're convinced we can't!

The first time I ran a seminar on creativity and memory for a Swedish company, this ability saved my bacon. After asking 15 people to introduce themselves – all Nordic names – one bright spark challenged me with the question, 'If you're going to teach us about memory, can you recall the names you have just heard?' Fortunately I could, even though I had only just switched on a little way into the introduction.

> *I learned for future reference a small tip that you can add to the above: if you have the luxury of a guest list beforehand, scan all the names two or three times.*

You now know that there are, for instance, three Olles, two Marys, etc. It makes the job of matching them a lot easier!

It's a simple, everyday example, but will awaken enough of your curiosity to think that failings of our memory and other mental functions, which we may have unfairly beaten ourselves up about, are simply because we haven't practised using the full power of our attention.

How often do we criticize ourselves for what we perceive to be our failing memory? If we come home from work and have left some important papers behind, we're likely to think that this is the beginning of the end – neurons dying, the sudden onset of aging and its inevitable decline. However, if you see what a group of nine-year-olds have left behind at school – bags, shoes, even trousers! – this doesn't result in them going home and feeling that they're losing their minds.

A practical way of realizing that your memory is better than you think is what I call three-minute re-thinks.

Just before you set off on that journey or leave for that meeting, sit still for three minutes, let the busyness subside, and just ask yourself inwardly what else you need. Most times the answer will come to you in that stillness. A very simple idea, but one that's obscured by the dust clouds of the daily rush.

The second element

To take a creative angle, we need to direct our attention to more tangential views of a situation, rather than using the mental battering ram of full-on force.

In the picture you can see a line in a box. Let's assume that it's indelible. How do you remove it?

One lateral solution is to add a much larger line that engages your attention more. Instead of focusing your attention on the existing problem, you have moved to another perspective that renders the original problem, if not completely solved, relatively insignificant.

Solving today's problems is paradoxically best achieved by introducing a *second element* that transcends the dominance of the original problem in your mind. If a room is dark, you don't try to remove the darkness, you just introduce the second element of light.

This, to me, is the true meaning of the old teaching story from the Sufi sage Mullah Nazrudin. It's a story I've often read, but to be honest it took me years to understand its significance. The Mullah – often portrayed as an idiot savant – is searching for his key in the road beneath a streetlight. When a friend asks him where he lost the key, he replies that it was in his house. When the puzzled friend asks why he is looking outside in the street at night Nazrudin points out that his house is dark and there is much more light under the streetlamp.

Anyone who takes this story literally is bound to be baffled. But of course, it's a teaching story about where to put your attention. It's not nonsense, but non-sense, which transcends a purely rational view.

Adopting the Nazrudin story intuitively doesn't mean looking for your key in the garden when you *know* it's in the house. The story is talking about bigger, more open-ended quandaries. The first step is therefore to stand back from what seems intransigent. This could be a literal step back: the poet Wallace Stevens said that sometimes all it takes is a walk around the lake. The 'light' in this case is partly the new perspective, partly the oxygen to your brain: although only about 3 per cent of the body's weight, the brain consumes 25 per cent of the fuel that's essential for problem solving.

Space and place

If it's a bigger topic than can be solved in a short walk, you may need to take yourself to a place where you are usually inspired (recall the Heineken copywriter going as far as Morocco for his solution). The 'yes, but' is often that 'there's no time'. It's difficult to remember the relative nature of time: for me one hour spent in the seclusion of my country hut often yields as many ideas as an afternoon in front of the computer, but strangely you need to be *in* that space in order to remember it!

So, where is your special space? If you don't have one, discuss with friends what they do, where they go when they have a pressing need to re-think something important.

You'll be surprised at some of the strategies people adopt: writer Will Self says he gets his best ideas in periods of long, monotonous motorway driving, and a colleague needs to take a long train journey if he's got a particularly difficult problem on his mind. If you're an active person try reading Bruce Chatwin's *The Songlines*, in which there are beautiful eulogies to the benefits of walking.

By taking yourself even briefly away from the 'darkness' of the difficulty you are allowing your mind to settle and begin to access the areas where the 'light' or solutions are found – in quieter, more expanded levels of your own mind. The process of incubating or mulling over works best when you are relaxed and can gain distance from the topic you are re-thinking.

Are you a critic or a creator?

It's very hard to be in both these states of mind at the same time. Creators are people who feel a compulsion to bring their ideas into being. It occurs best without interference from the little voice that says, 'This is no good', 'No one will be interested in this', etc.

Imagine what kept Emily Dickinson going, when over 1,700 of her poems were only found after her death. Only two were published, unagreed, in her lifetime.

This is one of the few cases in Re-Think *when I would advocate either/or rather than both/and thinking. Today are you a creator or a critic?*

There's always a little switch in your mind you can set to 'possible' or 'not possible'. Have you switched on to 'possible' mode?

But in cases where the indelible line really is indelible, such as a loved one's critical illness, moving towards the light means finding a way in your own mind to reframe the experience. Ellen Langer suggests practical strategies with her enlightened research. In one experiment she got participants to reframe their experience of hospitalization from a positive perspective: time to rest, reflect, get to see friends they hadn't seen for a long time and so on. The result was that they recovered sooner and in better spirits than a control group. It's a powerful example of *choosing* where to put your attention, a fundamental choice we make spontaneously many times a day between light and dark, criticism or creation, impossibility or possibility.

More profoundly, choosing where to put our attention actually reaches out to touch the apparently solid and physical world around us. It's been known in physics for nearly a century that the observer affects the observed. We can know either the velocity or position of a particle, an electron for example, but not both. The very act of paying attention causes the 'collapse of the wave function'. Similarly, when we pay attention to one matter over another we are creating fresh neural pathways in our brains by just bringing our awareness to bear.

The quality of our attention influences outcomes, so we should be careful what we put it on: whatever we focus on will grow. If it's fear and threat, then that will grow. In this sense, the police will always see increasing crime even when it's in decline, doctors will see a threatening disease despite health levels improving, and so on. Putting attention on the second element means not having your mind overshadowed by what is and has been, but drawn towards what can be.

> *'What we put our attention on grows!'*

RE-THINK NO. 10: TAKING A BAT'S VIEW

As a speaker and coach on creativity to organizations around the world, I've sometimes adopted the persona of a bat to help people redirect their attention more creatively. Bats, as you know, enjoy sleeping upside down during the daytime, giving them an upside-down, but quite fresh, perspective on life.

Putting our attention on an upside-down view of a problem gives us a whole range of new ideas. This is sometimes described as zigging while others zag.

Take, for instance, the common cliché that *people are an organization's greatest resource.* The bat's view is the reverse:

> *Organizations are people's greatest resource.*

Let's get this clear once and for all: organizations are a man-made fiction invented in order to achieve what individuals cannot do alone. If they are to become places that allow ordinary people to achieve extraordinary things, we have to turn our mindset inside out and start truly valuing the individual's higher needs.

In one-to-one coaching I encourage people to treat their organization as a university. Not the kind where you sit around drinking and playing music (though that's not an entirely bad idea), but one where you are hungry for new knowledge, exciting assignments and life-enriching experiences.

Another cliché that appears to make sense is when people say they need to:

'Implement ideas faster.'

The bat's view, of course, is to urge people to go slower. This is because I often hear 'We have great ideas – we just don't implement them fast enough.' This is misplaced confidence in the quality of the ideas. My experience is that if the ideas were so exciting and groundbreaking in the first place, they would naturally infuse the actor with a passion to see them brought to life.

Today it seems heretical to 'go slow'. But many heresies are great rethinks! Great ideas, like a fine wine, take time, or at least their own natural rhythm to mature. This is one of the tenets of the rapidly developing Slow Movement, which encourages us to eat, drink, think, and *be.* Not in a sluggish manner, but in a way that finds the right rhythm or speed for any activity.

Throughout the world there are a number of *Citta Slow.* The movement originated in Italy in the 1980s, encouraging whole cities of people to live in a more harmonious way with their surroundings. Eating food in the right season, grown in the immediate region, and taking time for meals together, leads to creative discussion and a better quality of life. The meal I had in the birthplace of this movement, Bra in Piedmont, was not only satisfyingly produced from local, in-season ingredients, it also tasted great and didn't take hours to cook.

Slow down

Using a snail for its logo, the Slow Movement is one of those quiet cultural revolutions that focuses on resisting fast food and the decline in quality of life that comes with it. So it also rejects the ethos of the high-velocity, urgency-driven life.

When you are considering what you need to give more importance to in your life, you may find these words from the Slow Food manifesto insightful:

'We are enslaved by speed and have all succumbed to the same insidious virus: Fast Life, which disrupts our habits, pervades the privacy of our homes, and forces us to eat Fast Foods.

'To be worthy of the name, Homo Sapiens should rid himself of speed before it reduces him to a species in danger of extinction.'

Staying with food, the highly successful YO! Sushi Japanese restaurant chain is based on typical bat's thinking. The food serves itself to you on small conveyer belts, which allow you to see immediately what you are choosing. If you look around you, you will see everywhere examples of innovations that are successful simply because they go against the main current of 'thinking as usual'.

So, whatever you are thinking about, turn it upside down, take the unusual and unthought-of angle. The bat's view.

Sometimes the mind can be opened by just reversing the words you are using. For instance, we're all familiar with focus groups and the rather predictable middle-of-the-road solutions they generate. In true bat's style, creative design group IDEO often works with *un*focus groups to help its customers. For instance, to explore ideas about sandals, they gathered together an artist, a body builder, a podiatrist, and a shoe fetishist! *Un*focusing can make a big difference in what you pay attention to.

The vital thing with taking a bat's view is not to be too literal about reversing the situation; creative re-thinking means fluidity of thought, so don't worry if the first few times you try this it seems a bit 'clunky'! What you are doing is tricking the mind out of its tendency to categorize in a rigid way, allowing you to approach the problem from a fresh, more open viewpoint.

Allowing the bat's perspective into your brain is often not a conscious process. Professor Martin Seligman was president of the American Psychological Association in 1997 when he had an epiphany gardening with his daughter Nikki. She commented to him that she had stopped being a whiner when she was five, and added, 'If I can stop whining, you can stop being a grouch'.

Instantly he realized that in over 100 years of psychology little had been said about happiness, goodness, and fulfilment. For every 100 psychology papers focusing on anxiety or depression, only one looks at a positive human trait.

He has now raised millions of dollars in research funds and applied the best empirical techniques to the study of what he calls Authentic Happiness. His work may well turn out to be a valuable reversal of what many people take as given – that psychology is only about problems.

There's a deeper mindset that Seligman and others are tackling here. 'Of the six universal emotions, four – anger, fear, disgust, and sadness

– are negative, and only one, joy, is positive. (The sixth, surprise, is neutral.)'[7]

The second element or solution is, in a deep sense, a form of memory. Inventing is literally remembering that there is another way, if only we can bring our attention to it and let in the light.

A final word from the bat. There is too much emphasis today on people being 'professional'. Frankly, I'm tired of dealing with jaded professionals who can give me 101 reasons why my request is not possible. But I'm touched by inspired amateurs, who, if they don't know the answer will find someone who does. Remember that 'amateur' comes from the Latin root, *to love.* Passionate people who love what they do. Long live the amateur.

RE-THINK NO. 11: FAMILY RITUALS

A major complaint in family life is the absence of quality attention given to the people we *say* we value the most. But this section isn't intended merely to make you feel guilty – here are some ways of paying attention that will enrich your daily life.

Hellos and goodbyes

In a time when most of us come and go so often, saying goodbye and hello on autopilot may seem like a small thing, but if you take others for granted they will start to do the same with you. When we're busy, the tendency is to lose our powers of discrimination and 'objectify' others. Kissing your loved one is unconsciously on the same list as remembering your car keys and mobile phone. You're simply not paying attention!

---

[1] *Time Magazine*, January 17, 2005, p. 37.

A gloomy reason for not taking the other for granted is that this parting *may* be the last one. But assuming – as most of us do – that this is not the case, remember how the way you left someone you care for can tinge your whole day with a small shade of regret.

So in your goodbye take a 3-minute re-think to be really present and acknowledge the importance of this small ritual. Touching is as significant as words.

What of our rituals of homecoming? It's sometimes said that the one thing we learn from experience is that we don't learn from experience, and nowhere is this more true than in our re-entry to home life. We know intellectually that the tone of the first few moments when we greet our loved ones can set the pattern for the whole evening. Or even the weekend! It's not a new idea but, like you, I'm capable of forgetting this. Frequently!

If you've been using your analytical faculties at work, your first instinct on coming home is to switch off or switch over from this mode, perhaps to 'veg out', watch TV or listen to music. The one who has been at home may have been wrestling with an insurance claim, leaking tap or truculent child. *They* want you to attend to these matters, to shed some of the load they've been carrying all day.

This re-entry time is a buffer zone – we all need to learn, or remember, rituals to get through this period as harmoniously as we can. I know a man who stops his car a mile from home to practise 20 minutes of meditation; his partner quickly noticed how he'd shed much of the frustration of the day before he walked through the door. Those of us out in the real world (a dangerous euphemism which demonstrates how we've come to value work over home life) are often unconscious of the monkey we're carrying on our back when we walk in.

The solution has to be unique to your relationship, but awareness of the different rhythm of the other is the starting point. My examples may make you cringe, but they will help you re-think your own patterns.

Music is an obsession of mine, and so before too many words are exchanged we often play something great (a *totally* subjective concept) and have a family dance together. The fact that apparently I cannot dance (hotly disputed by me, but we'll let that pass) is irrelevant – touching is as important as the moves.

Of course, life is more fluid than this daily example, and absences are frequently longer for many of us than a mere eight hours. Try calling the person you care about and leave a message that may be brief, but is all about the positive feelings you have for them.

Easy? No. You'll be tempted to just add a little line about the insurance or the car tax, but don't. Unless of course the kids have left home or you've just been fired. I often save some of these pleasant messages on my mobile, and if I'm away I listen to them at the start of the day. It's simply putting your attention on what's important, a small boost to help you through the day.

Winning bread, sharing bread

Our world has been turned upside down in an unhealthy way. Instead of working to be able to eat, we now eat to give us fuel for work.

We're all familiar with the fragmented meal times that have become the norm in so many families. The kids take a pizza to the TV room, the breadwinner (or often the breadwinner*s*) arrive home at different times, and the whole affair spreads out over more than one room and several disjointed hours. What's the point of 'winning bread' if you can't enjoy it? Or, in family life, enjoy it *together*?

David is a hard-working schoolteacher whose one household rule is that evening meals are to be taken together whenever possible. In his family that means *making* it possible. You may have to work at this by not allowing TV, PCs, or PlayStations during this time. Conversation about the day is encouraged, and to be at dinner with his family is to enjoy a wider range of topics than you're likely to see on 'prime time' television. For his family, this *is* prime time – a chance to argue, laugh and, above all, reconnect.

To his credit, he shares cooking duties with his partner, Alison, and of course the kids help. If this all sounds too Disney, it isn't. The usual everyday dramas, upsets and inevitable distractions are all there, but there is one family rule that is adhered to scrupulously – no telephone calls (or children twiddling with their mobiles) are allowed.

Don't get the idea that David is a stern Victorian patriarch or a SNAG (Sensitive New Age Guy). He's quite likely to finish his evening at the local pub with the guys after marking the homework. But mealtime is sacrosanct, and after initial armed resistance from the two children and some continuing guerrilla warfare ('Can't I play the new Slipknot album now?') they have come to accept this ritual as the norm.

Why not make it a weekly ritual (start with what's realistic) to have a proper family meal together in a way that you're all fully present.

I have focused very much on everyday rituals as a way of enriching and giving a shape to the staccato, shapeless lives so many of us lead. It would take another book to describe the larger rituals that have largely disappeared from our lives: the celebration of achieving womanhood or manhood, great successes, failures, bereavements and so on. But by putting our attention on the small, the stuff that appears to be beneath our intellectual radar, we start to find a more natural rhythm in our lives. This is particularly necessary in family units that aren't traditional but 'blended' with offspring from previous relationships.

Family journals

My family is sporadic at creating a journal of holidays or journeys we have undertaken, but it's a wonderful way of capturing shared experiences. The journals we make – begun with enthusiasm, rarely finished, but memorable none the less – are much more powerful records than the mindless photo albums that are a more passive reminder. Our seven-year-old produced a very creative journal record of a recent trip to India. A mixture of describing places and people in sketches, words, postcards and, yes, the odd photograph. This develops her ability to appreciate and reflect, and to be able to share her adventures with friends.

We have American friends who do this to a level our more disorganized clan will never be able to emulate. Every train ticket, receipt and business card of people they have met is neatly glued in strict chronological sequence into a leather-bound book. You don't have to be this (shall we say) *precise* for it to become a worthwhile family ritual.

Just make a journal with whatever old notebook you happen to have on you. But do it. Children love to contribute.

It also helps you understand more of their inner response to the over-stimulation many parents subject their offspring to.

Putting your attention on your wider family

A more profound re-think is to consider '*Who* are my family?' A journalist friend was asked for a loan by someone he knew well. His first reaction was to think that if it were his brother, he'd lend the money. A few days later he was drinking his morning coffee when it suddenly struck him that he had developed a very narrow view of 'family'. Many of us will know our friends longer than the partner we are now married to, and although he is happily married, he realized that friends are also his family – a wider community that we are bonded to almost as much as to our blood relatives. He made the loan.

The Indian sage Yogananda warned about the narrowing of boundaries that comes by thinking of family as 'we four, and no more'. As a re-think on the nuclear family there's a Sanskrit expression that says:

Vasudhaiv Kutumbakam – 'The world is my family.'

When I was married for the second time, we didn't have any prenuptial agreements about material things, but we did make a conscious agreement that our family life would always be inclusive of others. Now I'm often the only token English person in the family.

We don't always live up to this high ideal of treating the world as our family, but the intention has had a powerful effect on our life together and contributed to the rich diversity of people I'm likely to find in my house when I come home.

Time to re-think who is in your family ...

RE-THINK NO. 12: THERE'S NO PRESENT LIKE THE TIME

Being cash rich and time poor seems to be a peculiarly modern problem. And how we spend our time tells us a lot about what we value. Given that time is one of the great perceived scarcities, how can we re-think our attitudes towards how we use it and make sure that what's important gets the most attention?

This was a fashionable subject 20 years ago when time-starved delegates would emerge from a seminar on time management clutching their organizers or 'black bibles'. Today it's BlackBerries, but the concept of *managing* time seems to be as elusive as ever.

The essence of those programmes was to carve out time for yourself. For me, in daily periods of meditation, this means taking the advice one stage further as my two periods of stillness during the day are a way of contacting my self – but Self spelled with a big S.

The first step is to understand the *value* of time. It's interesting how much financial language is used when we talk about time: we talk about 'saving' time and 'spending' time. But the one thing we can't do is hoard it.

My shorthand for old ideas coming back into vogue again is to say 'Righteous Brothers!' There is a new record-buying generation every five years and you can't go wrong if you update a Righteous Brothers hit.

This can be a useful re-think in your own area of interest: what ideas from five years ago could be usefully revisited and re-released?

Let me do the same with time management.

Important, but not urgent

Here's the one-minute course on time management. Many years ago, a writer, Edwin Bliss, described categories of time use that are still relevant today. We spend our time on activities that are:

- Important and urgent
- Urgent, but not important

  and finally

- Important, but not urgent

Naturally, we hope to be putting our attention on things that are important *and* urgent, but find our time 'stolen' by what we perceive as being urgent but not important. How many times at the end of a busy day or week do you think, 'Where did my time go and why didn't I get down to what's really most important?'

Very few people sit down at the end of a week and celebrate what they *have* done – our attention tends to go to beating ourselves up for what we *haven't* done.

> *An important re-think is to develop a ritual for celebrating and enjoying what you have done.*

Often, it takes someone else to be the catalyst for this. A partner or friend to sit down with and get you to congratulate yourself for what you have achieved. Otherwise you are into a cycle of punishing yourself and never enjoying the fruits of your labour. And the health hazard is that you will want to press the button inside that tells you to *try harder*. Next week I'll get up an hour earlier, put in more sweat, and then the problem will be solved. You have set the bar at an impossibly high level, ensuring you will always feel a lack of fulfilment and self-worth.

The attitudinal shift that will make us feel we are spending our time more valuably means making space for the last category of time use, those things which are *important, but not urgent*. There's a gap between what we say we value and how we use our time. I've often asked a group whether spending time with close friends is important. Naturally they all say yes. Then I ask them how much enjoyable time they have had with their friends recently, and how many people they care about do they owe a phone call, email or letter to? Nearly everybody puts up a guilty hand.

It's being sucked into too much *urgency* that has stolen this gift of what is *important*. We are all in danger of being drawn into the mania for speed (now upgraded to 'velocity') at the expense of quality of life.

The kinds of things that people tell me they need to give more time to in their lives are:

- Relationships – partner, friends, family
- Creating the future rather than coping with the effects of the past
- Learning new skills
- Pursuing a personal passion
- Writing the book they always wanted to

Of course, there's always something more urgent to do. I recall a very evocative cartoon that describes a person going through the stages of life – starting at school, getting married, having children, growing old, and eventually being carried off in a coffin. At each stage they are saying 'I'm not ready for this'. It's possible to lead a whole life in this way.

The trick is to turn what's really important into something urgent.

Personal pleasures, contacting old friends, learning new skills, and creating the future rather than being trapped by the past are all worthy subjects for this. Also, it's when you are most urgently driven that you need to schedule a certain amount of diary time for pleasure. When you are really pressured, it's the time to plan some bliss, enjoyment or excitement into your schedule.

What's a day for?

Interestingly, it's two friends who have had heart attacks who seem to understand most what a day is for. They take little for granted and have really learned to enjoy every small moment. One of their slogans might be the line from the song, *I get all the news I need on the weather report.*[8]

Living fully

'It's only when we truly know and understand that we have a limited time on earth – and that we have no way of knowing when our time is up – that we will begin to live each day to the fullest, as if it was the only one we had.'

Elisabeth Kübler-Ross

How you start the day often determines the rhythm that follows you through the rest of it. Imagine the perfect start to your day. It may involve exercise, a walk, meditation, playing a musical instrument or being in the garden. How often do you achieve this? 'Well begun is half done' is an old English phrase, and that applies to a day more than anything.

When you are able, try not to make an alarm clock your first image of the day. I was very taken by actress and writer Shirley MacLaine who describes how she doesn't take calls before a certain time of day, preferring to be half an hour in a glorious shower, and then careful about the first conversation she has after that.

You may think that this sounds a bit precious and OK for a film star, but I've found it can be done, though it may need discussion and cooperation with those you live with.

---

[8] Simon and Garfunkel, 'The Only Living Boy In New York'.

Put your attention on creating that perfect start at least once this week and see how it affects the quality of your day.

Let's finish with a more spiritual view of what a day is for from the Persian poet Rumi:

> *Days are sieves to filter spirit, reveal impurities, and too, show the light of those who throw their own shining into the universe.*[9]

---

[9] *Unseen Rain, Quatrains of Rumi*, John Moyne and Coleman Barks, Threshold Books, 1986, page 4.

re-think five

Co-creation

A true combination of minds has created some of our best re-thinks. This is co-creation.

Would John Lennon and Paul McCartney have been as successful as individuals? We will never know, but it seems clear that the contribution of McCartney's natural melodic instincts with Lennon's acerbic intensity translated into uniquely memorable music. Would Crick, the co-discoverer of the double-helix of DNA, have created as well without the assistance of Watson? Or can we imagine a Gilbert without his Sullivan, a Rodgers without a Hammerstein?

Creative fighting

Here is Richard Rodgers recalling his work with lyricist Larry Hart: 'When the immovable object of his unwillingness to change came up against the irresistible force of my own drive for perfection the noise could be heard all over the city. Our fights over words were furious, blasphemous and frequent, but even in their hottest moments we both knew we were arguing academically and not personally.'

Michael Schrage, *No More Teams,*
Currency Paperback, Doubleday, 1995.

All of these relationships exhibited a strong degree of creative tension, sometimes even antipathy. The glue that kept these individuals creating together appears to be made of two ingredients:

- A basic level of trust or respect (not the same as liking the other).
- The ability to produce something together that couldn't be achieved alone.

A question of trust

To work together effectively with another you need trust. Trusting is often based on liking, but not necessarily: there are a few people I trust and can create with, but they're not always those I like the most. A critical decision for many people considering starting a venture or a project with another is whether they can trust the other person. If, for instance, two men are creating something together and they have female partners, my advice is simple – ask the women! I've observed many working partnerships that are somewhat rocky, and in nearly every case it's the woman who has the clearer perception about whether the other is to be trusted and with what. Too often the men are in denial – 'he's my mate' – while the woman sees the imbalances and relative strengths of the two with more objectivity.

When I consider doing some creative work with someone new I usually take along a female colleague who can assess the other with a cool objectivity I value. The only times I've made mistakes have been when I wasn't able to do this, or ignored the advice.

Trust is of course *won* rather than assumed. (Or assumed at your peril.) A practical device is to set the other some small task – a low-risk one

– to see how it works out, and how you feel about the working relationship. You don't want to re-mortgage your house based on the hope that it will all turn out right!

There's a simple equation that describes how trust is won:

$$\text{TRUST} = \frac{\text{INTIMACY} \times \text{CREDIBILITY}}{\text{RISK}}$$

This comes from a team game – Red/Blue – which tests trust between two groups, but we can apply it just as readily to two people attempting to create together. *Intimacy* means you have got under the skin of another, and that you play together as well as work together and can discuss your problems, beliefs and hopes. *Credibility* is established by how you perform in bringing an idea to fruition, how your styles complement each other and how you support the project. Your credibility stems from what you do, not what you say.

Finally, the bigger the *risk*, the more important it is to have the other two ingredients established. If there's not much risk – for example arranging a tennis match – I don't need to have the same degree of intimacy with you as if we are starting a new venture together. You will have to assess these ingredients intuitively as well as rationally.

Ingredients for successful co-creation

There are four further essential elements for co-creating successfully with others. These apply to teams as well as pairs.

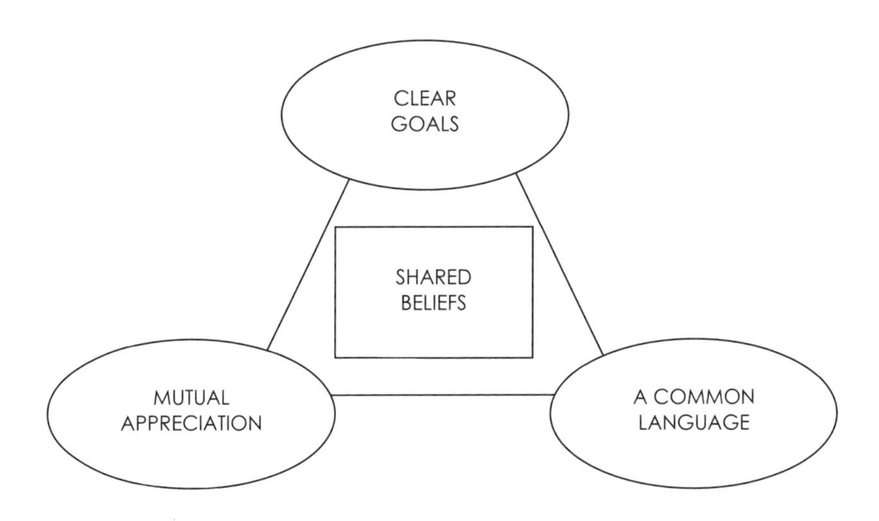

The core is *shared beliefs*. Note this doesn't mean *identical* beliefs – that's unlikely to produce the creative spark – but it does mean you have discovered what your creative nature is for, what you hope you can achieve through it, and the challenges you want to apply it to. The way in which you agree on this is as varied as the personalities involved. But aired and discussed it must be.

Clear goals is a more obvious ingredient. Less obvious is that these will change, perhaps weekly, and the sign that you haven't continued to discuss this will be that the word 'assume' comes up more in conversation – 'Oh, I *assumed* we were trying to …' I've been involved in project groups that begin to exhibit this tendency, and the only solution is to stand back from the day-to-day and thrash it out until you have a new agreed direction that you all *broadly* agree to.

It's not surprising that many creative partnerships fail because both parties become overwhelmed by the day-to-day demands and are working to a different set of assumptions. This is less surprising in large organizations – which we could describe as more than four people! – where you have the dubious pleasure of being able to blame others. With a small group you only really have yourself to point at.

Mutual appreciation is critical. This encompasses trust, which hopefully by now you've tested enough to know it's a working proposition.

From time to time it's useful to tell the other how much you appreciate something they did.

You have to find your own way of doing this – after a while it can be non-verbal. As much as anything your appreciation will be shown in the way you talk to others about your creative partner: if you have real appreciation this should extend to not putting them down behind their back. Oh, all right, a little grumbling may be in order, but it shouldn't be anything you couldn't say to their face.

Finally, a *common language* is vital. To an extent this will be driven by the arena you're working in, whether it's the arts, sports or business, but I mean something rather more unique and intimate. Jokes, shared references, a kind of shorthand that evolves. Even mocking the world together can be a form of bonding that reinforces your identity as a couple with a unique purpose. The creators of the jazz-rock group Steely Dan, Walter Becker and Donald Fagen, paid their musical dues in their early years as backing musicians to Jay and the Americans. Some nights they would play a song in a different key to see if the group noticed – they didn't. This was a way of asserting their joint identity as a creative twosome through the shared language of humour.

I remember having my hair cut in the City of London while a close friend I work creatively with came in for a chat. The hairdresser finally remarked that she hadn't understood a single word we'd said, and that we talked in a bizarre code. This was a revelation to us – years of working closely together meant that we were able to use shorthand for many topics, people or even ways of thinking, based on shared experiences, triumphs, disasters and jokes. Cherish this personal language you develop. It can be a short cut to creative solutions.

A question of style

Not all people are creative or solve problems in the same way. For instance, you may require a large amount of data, need very clear goals, and think in a focused way, drilling deeply into the problem. Your partner may prefer the big picture, become impatient with detail, and flit from one task to another at an alarming rate.

Many attempts have been made to describe and label different styles of thinking. Philosopher Isaiah Berlin categorized thinkers as foxes or hedgehogs. The fox has a tendency to think about many things, whereas the hedgehog thinks deeply about one thing. More commonly we tend to define the style of others as 'like me/not like me'. Despite the theory that different but complementary styles are needed to light the creative spark, in practice *my* big ideas may seem woolly and unclear, while *your* attention to detail may appear cautious and limiting. This gap in perception may hinder the lighting of that spark.

Fortunately, there is a more useful and insightful approach to understanding our own and others' style preferences. The Adaption-Innovation (A-I) Theory is based on the rigorous and extensive research of British academic Dr Michael Kirton.

Kirton's A-I theory assumes that we all have the capacity for creativity but express this in different ways. This is what he means by style – *how* we use our problem-solving talents, as opposed to how much creativity we have.

Everyone's style can be viewed on a continuum from highly adaptive – preferring to do existing things *better* – to highly innovative – preferring to tackle problems *differently*. There's a very accurate psychometric inventory, which captures our own style preference, the KAI. The inventory needs to be administered by someone fully trained in its use and assessment (details in 'Re-think resources' in the Appendix). However, here are simple descriptions of the style tendencies from highly adaptive to highly innovative. Although we all have a definite preference, we will almost certainly have elements of adaptor *and* innovator within us.

An extremely adaptive style tends to solve problems in these ways:

- Precision, reliability, efficiency, prudence, methodicalness, conformity.
- Resolving problems rather than finding them.
- Seeking solutions to problems in tried and understood ways.
- Challenging rules cautiously, when assured of strong support.
- Reducing problems by improvement and greater efficiency with maximum of continuity and stability.

This style is essential to the functioning of any institution, but occasionally high adaptors need to be 'dug out' of their own system.

At the other end of the scale is the innovative style:

- Seen as undisciplined, thinking tangentially, approaching tasks from unexpected angles.
- They discover fresh problems and avenues of solution.
- Are catalysts to settled groups, challenging assumptions, irreverent of consensual views.
- Often challenge rules, have little respect for past custom.

They are ideal in unforeseen crises, or better still to help to avoid them, if they can be controlled!

Is our style fixed?

It may be hard to acknowledge that we have a stable style preference that doesn't change much from our teens to old age. The self-help industry advocates that anyone can achieve anything so surely we can just don an adaptive hat when faced by a solution that seems to require a more detailed approach, and then put on our innovative hat when we're looking for a genuinely new solution?

But just as we have a preference for using one hand, eye or ear, it's natural that experience, training and heredity has accustomed us to a method of problem solving.

What *does* change, at least if we develop greater self-awareness and maturity, is our *coping* behaviour. This is the ability to act, at least for short periods of time, in our own approximation of a different style.

One of the main benefits of understanding our style is to be open enough to see where another person's very different approach can complement our own.

Naturally, the theory is more complex as these are extreme ends of a continuum. So don't stereotype yourself as one or the other – the main value of the theory for creating with others is *knowing whether you are more or less adaptive or innovative than another.* If I am even slightly more adaptive than you, I may perceive you as taking unnecessary risks and not thinking things through. If the situation is reversed, I am likely to see you as unnecessarily cautious, slower and needing more structure than I do.

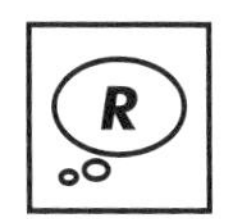

One way to test this out is to think about someone you know very well – perhaps a work colleague or your partner. Are they more or less adaptive than you? Think about specific tasks you do together, like organizing the family holiday. Does one of you just have the big idea – 'Let's go to Spain' – while the other spends two months making the detailed arrangements? It's not guaranteed, but you should be able to guess from this which of you is more innovative and which more adaptive. Swapping roles occasionally might save the marriage!

Kirton's research bears out that we develop a stable preference early on in life, and although we may operate for brief periods in what we believe to be another style (described as coping behaviour), even the big picture innovator will have to get down to some level of detail to bring an idea into being.

The implications of KAI theory are far-reaching. In education it's clear that if learning is tailored in a way that doesn't fit well with your preferred style, you won't get too far. Many – though not all – entrepreneurs have a preference for a more innovative style of learning, which is why so many fall out with authority and resist what they perceive to be narrow and over-structured types of schooling. The theory also explains why those with a relatively adaptive style tend to dislike unstructured methods of idea generation. They aren't fans of what's loosely called 'brainstorming'.

I certainly wish I'd known more about my style when I was younger. As an innovator, it's clear in hindsight that some of the career decisions I took could have been better informed with this information. The most practical use I make of this knowledge is to treat my relatively adaptive or innovative clients in appropriate ways. For instance, if they are highly innovative, I'm likely to get only the briefest of briefings before getting on with the job, and may need to compensate by being over-focused on the logistics and practicalities myself. In contrast, if they are far more adaptive, I will try to produce a level of detail and structure in my proposals that frankly has me yawning after a few minutes. I even have a file that's labelled 'adaptive' containing detailed histories of my previous projects.

Reaching out and tuning into the different style of another is one of the most important re-thinks you can do when co-creating.

Re-thinking innovation

One of Kirton's great insights is to reclaim the real meaning of the word innovation, which is commonly confused or used interchangeably with the term creativity. Innovation means, literally, 'newness', whereas much of the creativity we see around us is the result of creative adaption. The internal combustion engine was undoubtedly a great innovation – arguably what we have seen is a century of refinements or adaptions ever since.

So when many leaders call on their people to be more innovative, currently a very sexy word, they need to think more carefully about what they are asking for. It's worth remembering that innovations initially tend to be less efficient than existing methods. The first steam-powered vessels were less efficient than the sailing ships they competed with, and the first motor cars a slower method of travel than a coach and horses. Put in a new computer system and in the short term you probably can't even do the basics: you hope, as with all innovations, that there will be a step change in performance once you've got through the initial chaos.

Technology is one field that is crying out for more adaption and less innovation. We may talk about road rage, but a more pervasive curse of 21st Century life is computer rage. If you've never thought of throwing your laptop out of the window, you're either very technically savvy, or deeply repressed.

What most of us want is for the technology to work as reliably as, say, a land line telephone or TV. There will be a huge market in the future for truly idiot-proof mobile phones and PCs. Currently, it's as if the whole human race is involved in an unwitting act of co-creation to help technology manufacturers make their machines work. No wonder writer Douglas Adams observed, 'Technology is the name we give to something that doesn't quite work yet.' In this way, innovation is both a blessing and a curse.

Re-thinking can stem from fruitful collaborations between adaptors and innovators, as in the invention of the famous Bailey Bridge during the Second World War.

Brigadier Stair of the Engineer Corps found himself looking at a design sketched out literally on the back of an envelope. Collecting a team, he set out to turn this brilliant spark into the wartime bridge named after the innovator who had drawn the initial picture.

The Brigadier steered the idea through all the necessary committees. He was a member of all the key ones and made sure that the Allies had a bridge that could be assembled, mostly by amateur manpower, in a fraction of the time that was previously possible.

This is a great example of how an innovator can combine with an adaptor to create something neither of them could have done alone.

Teams and KAI

Put simply, there are two types of creativity:

- Type 1: *Adaption* – improving, refining and developing what already exists.
- Type 2: *Innovation* – generating new and different solutions.

Both types are equally valuable; which you rely upon depends to a great extent on your own preference and the kind of challenge you are facing. I often use the KAI inventory to paint a picture of a group's preferred style before helping them to work more creatively together. One of the least successful pieces of team coaching I did was with the board of an investment company where the predominant style was highly innovative. Innovators often need to work harder at being team players; they prefer to rock the boat, challenge the rules, and get bored easily. Put a group of them together and the meeting may be sparky, but there's a great chance of it going off at a tangent at any time.

This group told me they were going to communicate a new organizational structure to their people. Now, what a relative innovator thinks is a sufficient level of detail may seem vague and lacking in thought to a more adaptive person. In fact, high innovators seem to believe that if they've had an idea, it must be immediately apparent to others! My client rang me two months later to say they almost had a revolution on their hands: the degree of detail and structure they had communicated left people totally confused about their new responsibilities. The team needed someone with a relatively more adaptive style to translate their ideas into something detailed, sequential, and structured. In other words, adaptive creativity.

In contrast, one of the most successful teams I coached was running a refinery. They had the project of taking out $80 million worth of costs without making any compulsory redundancies. This team had the complete range of styles, and most significantly, their boss was right in the middle. He played a very effective 'bridging' role between the more adaptive and more innovative tendencies of the team so that sessions together became a truer meeting of minds. The team went on to achieve their goals.

Specifically, the leader understood *and* valued both adaption and innovation. Drawing in the adaptive minds ensured continuity and the ability to follow things through, while tapping the innovator's minds helped to generate new and different solutions.

Anyone in a working group, but particularly the leader, has a duty to bridge between the different styles to make sure that both different *and* better solutions are fully explored.

Vive la difference

While greater awareness of your own style and the effect it has on others is critical, it's vital that you also develop greater *appreciation* for the contribution of others with different styles. Although we may theoretically acknowledge the need for complementary approaches – someone to dot your 'i's or to get you to see a new angle – in practice, and particularly under stress, it's much harder to do.

An innovator who has an adaptive boss may believe that he or she is required to provide far more detail than is necessary and may feel as if a strong brake is being put on more exciting and riskier ideas. Conversely, someone with a more adaptive style working for a relative innovator may become frustrated by shifting priorities and lack of a clear sense of direction. They may demand more structure and more tightly defined goals than the innovator is prepared or even able to provide.

You may be able to gauge your preferred style just by the way you read *Re-Think*. While there's always a danger of generalizing, if you have a relatively innovative style, you may prefer to skip and skim, perhaps thinking you've 'got' the idea even before you've read it! Innovators want everything to happen relatively quickly and are frustrated at not getting to the point. If you have a bias towards adaption, you may prefer to read from start to finish and require arguments to be clearly thought through. And, for the advice to be more practical.

RE-THINK NO. 13: BLUE THINKING

Blue/Red/Green

There's a highly effective shorthand for creative problem solving that I've used for many years with groups. It's originally the brainchild of creativity writer Mark Brown, though what I describe here is a simplified version of his model. We can condense what we know about group creativity into a language of just three stages, represented in the illustration below.

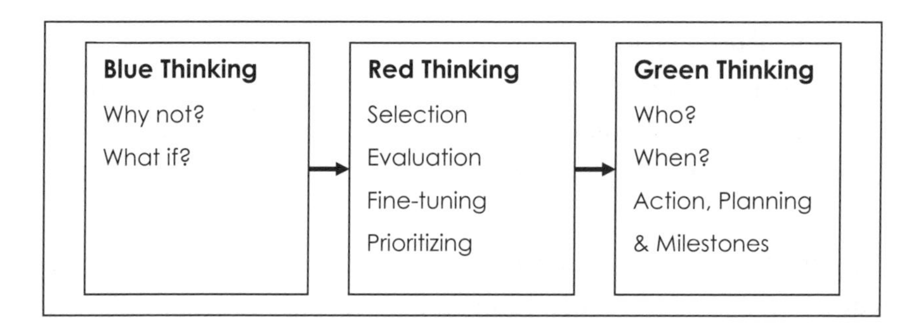

The colour scheme is very easy to grasp. Blue is for ideas – the sky's the limit.[1] Red is for stop (as in traffic lights), consider, refine and choose the best ideas you've generated. Green is for 'go': who is going to do what, by when, etc.

Seems straightforward, doesn't it? You generate some great ideas (blue), select the most likely winners (red) and then decide how to implement them (green). But in practice this is more complex.

A meeting of bodies in a room does not necessarily mean a meeting of minds. Some of us have a preference for 'blue' thinking and enjoy having idea after idea without any thought for the practical implica-

---

[1] Intended in a more practical way than 'blue sky thinking', which along with other ghastly business-speak, is brilliantly parodied in Lucy Kellaway's *Who Moved My BlackBerry?* Viking Paperback, 2005.

tions. Others are naturally attuned to 'red' thinking, wanting to go over an idea with a fine toothcomb even before it's fully developed, while 'green' thinkers can't believe why you just can't get on with it, and are all too aware of pressing deadlines. Their motto could be described as:

> *Ready!*
> *Fire!*
> *Aim!*

Or, in more extreme cases:

> *Fire!*
> *Ready!*
> *Aim!*

The trick is to allow sufficient time, energy and focus for each phase, which is where the shared language is so valuable.

The main enemy of really exploring fresh solutions is going red when you're meant to be in blue. Come again?

Well, let's say you're trying to develop an idea. It might be an old idea revisited or a breakthrough, 'deep blue' notion. Someone moves prematurely into the red phase by saying 'yes, but …' This immediately tends to kill the idea. *All great ideas are a triumph of 'why not? what if?' thinking over red or 'yes, but it can't be done' barriers to its development.*

The stereotypical way of thinking about 'blue' is that it's 'brainstorming'. This is quite wrong. Blue thinking means suspending your judgement, which tends to be clouded by past and limiting experience, for long enough to give birth to a new or better solution.

The red phase is valuable in that doubts can be expressed, but only when people know what it is they are doubting rather than demolishing an idea that they have not fully 'got' and are pre-judging. Similarly, the green stage enables an idea to find its expression in action, without which it is merely 'blue skying'. In practice the process is iterative – you go backwards and forwards and, given the infinite fluidity of human thought processes, one colour will bleed into another. But without this shared language you may find you are in a room where minds are locking horns or diverging in all kinds of unuseful ways.

Let's suppose you want to communicate some ideas to work colleagues – perhaps it's a status report on a project, some concerns you have about working practice or just a new idea you'd like to get a response to. You've decided to send an email and want to 'go blue' on the ideas to include. You've gathered two workmates to have a creative session on your idea.

Stop! Time out for a re-think. You've already decided on your *means* of communication – an email – and have therefore already narrowed your blue thinking into one channel of achieving the goal. In our colour language, you have 'gone green too soon'! This is where assumptions should be tested, and the most effective way is to keep going back in a childlike way to asking *why* and *what*: what's the real effect you want to produce, and why?

If, in the above example, you decide your purpose is to make a big impact on your colleagues with your idea, you could either:

1 think of alternative methods of engaging them (e.g. a breakfast meeting, time out in a pub or boat); or

2 hold back from deciding the method until you've gone blue on the content of the message.

How long should you spend on revisiting your real goal or purpose behind your creativity? Exactly this long: longer than you think.

The pull to 'get to green' – the action phase – is extremely powerful. But if you don't spend some time reflecting on your real purpose it will cost you time later. You will need to resist the pull towards 'green' or action if you want greater quality in thinking.

Guidelines for going blue

What matters as much as any process or technique used is the quality of interaction between you and others co-creating.

So here are the guidelines that groups I've worked with have found useful in remembering the overall philosophy and practice of blue thinking:

	WHAT	WHY
1	Record *all* ideas	Out of sight, out of mind!
2	Generate, don't judge	Often the best process is to have *lots* of solutions, eventually discarding the 90% that don't work
3	No 'yes, buts'	This assassinates *potentially* good ideas too early on
4	Think 'Why not?' 'What if?'	This encourages a group not to dismiss an idea merely because it seems shocking or impractical: the best ones often are, at first sight!
5	And, build and explore	Unlike brainstorming, this means you stay with a 'seed idea' proposed by another and help it to grow
6	Find the best environment for creativity	Can you really be relaxed with 2 metres of table between you and another? Get physically close and find the environment that works for you
7	Manage your energy level	When most groups take a break, it's half an hour too late. Eureka moments come in the gaps and when you stand back. Let go more often!
8	Have fun	Because in a relaxed state you're more open to ideas. Many a true word is said in jest

Give this list to your group, discuss, and agree which practices you most need to work on to co-create successfully.

RE-THINK NO. 14: A QUESTION OF STYLE

Awareness and appreciation of style – your own and others' – is key to creating successfully together. Kirton's theory doesn't propose, stable though your preference is, that it's most usefully viewed as an absolute. Its prime value is in knowing your style *in reference to others* you are working with.

If I am even slightly more adaptive than you, I may perceive you as taking unnecessary risks and not thinking things through enough. If the situation is reversed, I am likely to see you as unnecessarily cautious, perhaps slower and needing more structure than I see as warranted.

Although you need to do the KAI inventory with someone qualified you have probably got a rough sense by now of your own style in relation to people you know well: spouse, work colleagues, boss.

Here are some of the questions you can reflect upon in order to co-create more effectively with others:

- *How appropriate is my style for the challenges I am facing?* Do I need more structure (greater adaption) or do I need to challenge assumptions and let my thinking flow into new ways of looking at the problem (more innovation)?

- *How do I complement my own preference with the contribution of others?* In other words, find someone with the positive attributes needed for a more 'all round' approach to a problem.

- *If I'm in a team, what styles are missing?* Teams will adopt a way of reaching consensus that's most natural to them, tending to be around the average score for the group. Too much adaption and you may find you are grinding on in a very logical, but slow manner; too much innovation and you may be firing off ideas but failing to reach a conclusion.

- *How can I use the insights about my own style to resolve style conflicts I have had in the past?*

Considering the last question, I found that I was often falling out with a colleague who was relatively more adaptive than myself, not so much because of *what* we were doing, but *how* we were approaching a project. He would always require more detail and want to work in a thorough, sequential fashion. I would quickly become bored with what I saw as unnecessary checking and a much slower pace of working.

While understanding our KAI preferences wasn't quite a road to Damascus revelation, it did help us greatly to acknowledge and appreciate each other's contributions, strange and frustrating though the other style appeared. I would allow him the time and space he needed to work things through, while he became less of a 'yes, butter' and more receptive to my flights of fancy. The job got done more successfully than we'd have believed possible at the outset.

This is one of the greatest values of A-I theory: understanding how to communicate with someone with a different, even alien, style to one's own.

If someone is more adaptive, then give them more time to respond, stay with an idea and develop it instead of flitting on to the next one. Above all, respect their need for structure and clarity of purpose. Don't assume that having ideas for their own sake will be welcome.

> *Conversely, if the other is more innovative than you, get to the point quickly, make it exciting, and paint the big picture, tolerating what seems like a shorter attention span and a more haphazard way of working. Most of all, work at keeping your mind open to new, even shocking avenues of thought.*

Finally, remember the perceptual blind spot we all have: the belief that our world is – or should be – the same world that others see. Realizing this should allow in to your working practices different, complementary and potentially enriching ways in which others look at problems. This apparently simple re-think is the key to co-creating more effectively with others.

re-think six

Funny bones

The tricky part of writing about humour is that it's highly personal; what I find hysterical may leave you stone cold, and vice versa. Also, it's a subject that doesn't bear too much analysis. I once went to a lecture by a well-known professor of literature, investigating the development of the joke in the English novel, and lost the will to live after ten minutes. I recalled Woody Allen's line, 'Eternity is very long – especially towards the end.' Over-analysing humour is a little like the old metaphor of removing a spider's legs to study it better – the problem being that it just doesn't jump as well afterwards.

However, the intriguing parallels between humour and creativity makes it worth the risk. Where would we be without risk taking? And where would we be without rhetorical questions?

Arthur Koestler, a great writer on creativity, neatly encapsulated where humour fits in to the creative continuum, which he describes as ah! aha! haha!

- AH! (artistic creativity – how beautiful are those blues of Raphael!)

- AHA! (The scientific breakthrough – 'Aha! There's the double helix, James!')

- HAHA! (Humour in all its forms – as play, insight, surprise, observation, ridicule, satire, tomfoolery, slapstick, etc.)

The notion of 'serious play' is well known in the study of creativity, and its role in generating ideas is understood by scientists and artists alike. Physicist Richard Feynman made a breakthrough on the Dirac Equation just by observing how the Cornell University logo wobbled on a plate in the canteen. He said:

> *'It was effortless. It was easy to play with these things. It was like uncorking a bottle: everything flowed out effortlessly. I almost tried to resist it! There was no importance to what I was doing, but ultimately there was. The diagrams and the whole business that I got a Nobel Prize for came from that piddling around with that wobbling plate.'*[1]

Eastern philosophy describes existence itself as Lila Shakti, or the play of the Lord. Many holy men, such as the Dalai Lama, seem to have the faculty of laughing easily, even when they are talking about profound matters. In the West we have the archetype of the Jester and Shakespeare's fools. Many a true word *is* said in jest. Let's look at some of the different forms humour takes, and in the re-think section we'll apply these approaches to the art of creative thinking.

Effective surprise

Seeing a new creation often gives us a rush of surprise. From the striking sails of the Sydney Opera House to the strangely humanoid bottom of the Renault Megane. It's the same with humour. Here are two simple stories that work in this way.

> *We're all familiar with the famous words of Neil Armstrong, the first man on the moon, 'One small step for man – one giant leap*

---

[1] *Surely You're Joking, Mr Feynman: Adventures of a Curious Character*, Richard Feynman, Vintage Paperback, 1992.

> *for mankind.' What's been less known is that he added a phrase sotto voce, 'Over to you, Mr Blatsky.' When asked about this he would say it was private. But during a lecture tour of American colleges in 1995 he was quizzed about it again. After a pause he replied that now he could explain this as sadly Mr Blatsky had passed on. He explained how he had grown up next door to neighbours, the Blatskys. One day he heard an argument between them. Mrs Blatsky was shouting, 'Sex?! You want oral sex? You'll get oral sex when ... when that kid next door walks on the moon!' Over to you Mr Blatsky ...*

> *A story is told about an English football manager, Ron Atkinson. One of his players had been knocked out. The physio checked him on the field, then rushed back to the touchline to Ron to tell him that his player, although concussed, could run and play, but just couldn't remember his name. Ron responded, 'Well, tell him he's Pele and send him back on.'*[2]

With hindsight you can probably see how both stories were leading up to their conclusion. It's the same with creativity – a new solution looks logical when we look backwards. The skill is to be able to make this sudden leap, the discontinuity that isn't achieved by mere plodding incrementalism. In this way, both comedy and creativity can be seen as 'effective surprises'. The sudden leap can only be made on the *basis* of the logical part of the story, but the last step confounds and surprises this logic.

Upside-down perceptions

Re-thinks are often achieved by reversing our fixed point of view. This shakes up the component parts of the problem into a fresh configuration and we may see opportunity rather than obstruction. Pull may work better than push.

---

[2] *We, Me, Them and It: The Power of Words in Business*, John Simmons, Texere Publishing, 2000, pp. 198–9.

There's the story of an elderly Australian lady who was asked if she'd like to visit England. She thought about it for a while before replying, 'No, I wouldn't want to go there – isn't that where all the convicts come from?'

Similarly when the Channel Tunnel first connected England and France a UK newspaper ran a piece entitled 'CONTINENT NO LONGER ISOLATED'. Now this second story, although not as funny as the first, does shed light on a more serious point about perception. In fact, I used it as a *mea culpa* to help me out of a difficult spot when I was working with an Irish bank and described England as 'the mainland'. Without knowing the Gaelic for a faux pas, I had certainly committed one. Humour is a language we can use to creatively retrieve a lost position, and it's often more effective than pedestrian logic and self-justification.

No Bush gags

At the Edinburgh Festival in 2005, American comedian Dave Fulton remarked, 'I don't do Bush gags. Not while he's still speaking for himself.'

A colleague used this successfully when a client was querying his fees, pointing out that competitors could provide the same service for less. 'Well,' he said, 'that's good because we're never knowingly *oversold* – if someone else turns out to be more expensive than us, naturally we'll raise our fees to match theirs.'[3] After a pause the client laughed, and fees were never mentioned again.

---

[3] For non-UK readers, 'Never knowingly undersold' is a famous slogan of the well-respected retailer, The John Lewis Partnership. A phrase that's had to be slightly qualified with the advent of online retailers.

The English have a great love for this kind of thinking. A famous estate agent in London in the 1960s, Roy Brooks, would shock and entertain customers with the honesty of his advertisements. 'A brothel in Pimlico' is how he famously described one not so 'des res'. On an individual basis, this inverted thinking appears in the personal ads section of the *London Review Of Books*. Many of these are so eccentric and humorous that the magazine is publishing a book of them. I particularly like this one:

> *'Shake hands with Dalkeith, Midlothian! Official greeter and face of Dalkeith Cheese Festival, 1974, seeks woman to 50 who is no stranger to failure, debt-consolidating mortgages, and wool. Must enjoy beards and harbour contempt for any music that isn't Belgian jazz. Box 28/04.'*

Upside-down thinking is illustrated by an advertisement that Virgin Atlantic planned, but had to pull, around the time of the first Gulf War. It was for cheap fares from the Middle East to America. 'Cheap return flights to America – visit the US before the US visits you.'

Seeing the familiar in a fresh light

A great deal of re-thinking focuses on taking a familiar object and transforming it. Look at the myriad shapes, materials and colours you can buy a radio in today and you'll see how the dull old box has been transformed.

Similarly, humour shines a fresh light on the everyday. Advertisers know how to use this to good effect, as in the slogan, 'I thought Reading was a town in Berkshire until I discovered my local library.' (The town is pronounced *Redding*.)

Here are a few well-known words redefined by the team of the long-running BBC Radio series *I'm Sorry I Haven't A Clue*, the self-styled antidote to panel games:

Abacus – a Swedish swearword.

Accomplish – a drunken sidekick.

Dunderhead – a sculptor's delight in having done a significant part of the job.

Usury – Japanese for usually.

There's a whole book of these called *The Uxbridge English Dictionary*.[4] I can recommend this as a trigger for your own ability to play with words. It's an enjoyable and insightful way of not taking the obvious for granted.

Lugubrious American Steven Wright is like most great comedians in that he doesn't often do 'jokes' – the set pieces of comedy – but gives us a fresh slant on everyday sayings. When he's asked, 'Did you sleep well?' he replies, 'No, I made a few mistakes'. His response to the meaningless 'you can't have everything' is 'no … where would you put it?'

Or he takes a common phrase like 'It's a small world' and adds the line 'but I wouldn't want to have to paint it.' Individually these lines are hardly belly laughs, but as Wright builds up one slightly twisted take on reality on top of another, you find your perception pleasantly skewed and refreshed by the experience. It's as if he opens a gateway to a subtly different view, and develops in you the faculty of testing, checking and re-thinking many of the expressions we all use in a stereotypical way without thinking. In this way, humour helps you *think!*

---

[4] *Uxbridge English Dictionary (I'm Sorry I Haven't a Clue)*, Jon Naismith, HarperCollins, 2005. Reprinted by permission of HarperCollins Publishers Ltd. © Jon Naismith, 2005.

Eccentric British comedian Bill Bailey has a gift for this kind of humour. He describes the catalogue of low-price retailer Argos as 'the laminated book of dreams'. Then he explains why it's laminated: 'To catch the tears of joy'. I can't go into Argos and keep a straight face now.

Insight through humour

Comedy isn't all fantastical, unrelated to, or an excursion from real life. It can be used as a vehicle for ridiculing prejudice, hitting the mark in a way that rational arguments don't achieve.

There is a new crop of Muslim stand-up comedians in the UK who are brave enough to ridicule even the horrors of the age of terror. Paul Chowdry remarks that he never used to be able to get a seat on the train. 'Now I get the whole carriage, sometimes the whole network.'

Eddie Izzard is a brilliant raconteur who manages to convey some serious social comment in his hit-and-miss but often hilarious rants, a great deal of which are improvised. He's bi-sexual, which gives him plenty of material on prejudice to work with.

Commenting on the spurious claims of the National Rifle Association (NRA) that 'guns don't kill people – it's people who do', he adds pensively, 'but I think the guns help a bit.'

Irreverent American comedian Bill Hicks was doing a show in the South's Bible Belt. He was approached by two very large men after his show who said, 'We didn't like what you said in your show. We're Christians.' 'Then forgive me,' retorted Hicks.

To return to Steven Wright, here is a wonderful line of his that can help us think afresh about the concept of ownership: 'I have the planet's largest collection of seashells. I just like to leave them scattered on beaches throughout the world.'

Great comics are great observers, people who look at the world askance and perceive a different kind of truth. No wonder humour is thought of as potentially subversive and the focus for radical thinkers, mavericks and outsiders. And, increasingly, campaigners. Mark Thomas specializes in humour that addresses important social issues and targets specific companies to make injustices public. Last year it was Coca-Cola for their alleged mistreatment of workers in their Mexican plants. This year, who knows?

Organizational jesters

If the fools were so wise in Shakespeare, why not appoint one to work with your organization – company, school or hospital – as a check on hubris, excesses, injustice and plain foolhardiness? The cynic may claim that you already have too many comedians, but here we're talking about the wise fool who stops people taking themselves too seriously.

Surrealism

Surrealism is the juxtaposition of unlikely elements. In art it was defined as the meeting between an umbrella and a sewing machine on an operating table. This is one of the few descriptions I can remember unaided after many years, so there's a clue in surrealism for how to make your message stick.

Monty Python are the best-known modern champions of surrealism, at least in the English language. Everyone has their own favourite sketches or films. Mine include the competition to précis Proust (all six volumes of *A la Recherche du Temps Perdu*) in 15 seconds, the first round to be performed in swimwear and the second in evening dress, the housewives who discuss Jean-Paul Sartre in the laundrette and the famous philosophers' football match in which, after a lot of scratching of heads and pondering, Archimedes has the eureka experience that actually *doing something* and kicking the ball will win the game.

But the surreal also encompasses the real: Monty Python often parodied the stuffiness of the old English class system in skits like the Ministry of Silly Walks and the Upper Class Twit of the Year Show. By poking fun at the very medium they were using, BBC television, they made it difficult for stiff-lipped announcers to be hired again.

Perhaps the greatest genius of English comedy was Peter Cook, one of the four members of the satirical show of the early 1960s, *Beyond The Fringe*. He was a huge influence on Monty Python and much that followed. Here was an intelligent public school boy who founded England's first satirical stage club, the Establishment, started the magazine *Private Eye* and became a television, theatre and Broadway star while still in his 20s.

The title of his collected scripts is *Tragically I Was An Only Twin*, which gives you some idea of his way of looking at the world. Appearing in an old raincoat as his first great character, E L Wisty, he talks earnestly about forming a World Domination League, complains about having to beat Greta Garbo from his window at night, and describes how in a gallery of Reubens' paintings it's the bottoms, not the eyes, that appear to follow you around the room.

It may be possible to précis Proust, but you can't do the same with Peter Cook. I strongly recommend that you read his published scripts to liven up a dull evening.

Often the best and most surrealistic humour is improvised. It's an unpredictable flight of fantasy, apparently tangential to the matter at hand, but at its most successful when it adds something to our perception of reality.

Making you use your imagination

Sometimes humour leaves a gap for you to fill in your own interpretation. The work isn't all done for you, as in this final story.

A man walks into a pet shop and says he wants to buy a parrot. The shopkeeper points him to a fine specimen with beautiful plumage.

'How much is this one?'

'Two thousand pounds, sir.'

'Two thousand?! Why so much?'

'Well, he can sing every Beatles song word-perfectly.'

The man points to the next parrot with much duller feathers, and less of them.

'How much is this one?'

'Five thousand pounds, sir.'

'Five thousand!? Why? What can he do?'

'He can hum note-perfectly all of Mozart and Beethoven. Forwards *and* backwards.'

The man turns to the last parrot, almost bald and featherless. He is perched on a single leg and has only one eye.

'Well, how much is this one?'

'Thirty thousand pounds, sir.'

'My God! What can *he* do?'

'I have no idea, sir – but the other two call him the Master.'

RE-THINK NO. 15: AH-AHA-HAHA!

When I walk into a room where a team is working, it's almost possible to smell or touch the atmosphere. If they are looking strained and earnest they *could* just be very focused, but more often the sign that interesting thinking is going on is a buzz in the room, passion, energy and the relaxed attention that comes from being able to laugh easily. This is the mood of 'serious play'.

To explore how serious play helps us to re-think, let's make some connections with the modes of humour just described.

Effective surprise. In creative problem solving this means thinking of a shocking or unsayable departure from a straight, logical line to a solution. The most useful tools are 'what if?' or 'why not?' When thinking 'why not, what if' becomes a reflex – you've opened yourself to more possibilities. It's a way to prevent you from strangling your ideas at birth.

The main piece of advice given to people on creativity training is not to prejudge an idea. It's also the most difficult to follow, mainly because we *are* conditioned to judge: not just others, but ourselves. 'I can't say that', 'that's not relevant', 'that's just plain silly' is the kind of internal dialogue that often runs in our heads. It's all right to have arguments with yourself – it's when you start losing those arguments that you should start worrying.

In the worlds of both humour and creativity, there's no such thing as nonsense. At least not in the stage of *generating* ideas. In fact, if you're wanting to make an imaginative leap, non-*sense* is exactly what you want. Marc Andreeson, inventor of the first Internet browser, put it this way:

> *'If your goal is to create something new and big, you're going to have to do something that everybody else will laugh at – so that becomes the test. In other words, if it's something that makes everybody nod their heads and say, 'yeah, that makes sense', there are probably already a dozen people doing it.'*

This is an extreme point of view from a radical innovator, but at the risk of being contradictory we can still take the common*sense* from it by realizing that to make a breakthrough in thinking we need to contemplate the absurd, the ridiculous, or the unthinkable. *Then* we can work back to the original problem and integrate the practical and the achievable with our wilder, crazier ideas. It's much harder to start with what we *believe* to be practical because unconsciously we are limiting our ability to generate novel solutions. The gravity of today's 'reality' prevents our imagination from taking off and soaring.

Allowing for 'effective surprises' means:

- *If an idea just pops into your mind, try going with it and see where it leads you.*
- *Write down* any and every *solution you have with as little judgement as possible.*
- *If your mind can* entertain *an idea, it should be able to* express *it.*
- *Think of the most ridiculous solution,* then *water it down.*

Chances are you'll be pleasantly surprised at what's in your mind if you only give the ideas an outlet. Scribble them on a scrap of paper or tell them to someone who won't judge you for it.

One way of provoking your mind to think extremely differently is to entertain what you think is weird. Most great innovations are initially regarded as weird – that is, not part of thinking as usual.

> *So, make a list of the* weirdest *ideas you have for solving a problem, and extract from them what's different but useful. In re-thinking, weird is good.*

Upside-down perceptions. Entertaining and expressing, without censorship, surprising ideas that come into your mind can lead you into fruitful avenues of thought.

A well-known technique for achieving this is simply *reversal.* So if you are considering how to successfully launch a new idea, you might take time out to think how you could do it *un*successfully. Make a list and you'll naturally see many things to avoid. Now move your attention back to the original problem with this in mind and fresh ideas will stem just from working out ways to *avoid* these difficulties.

Similarly, if the discussion is about how to get closer to your partner: think about how to alienate or distance yourself, play with these notions and then return to the original formulation of the topic. Spontaneously a new crop of ideas will grow in this playful but serious state of mind.

We could call this either Bat's thinking or *zooming in/out.* Playfulness or humour allows you to adopt a wider-angle lens on the problem. Moving out to the wider view you will find that when you zoom in again you are seeing the situation from a new perspective.

This is where the analogy of a camera breaks down, because the brain has an almost infinite capacity to connect logically unrelated elements. While a camera *captures* a fixed image, the perceptual apparatus of the brain can be said to look behind it, see it in 3D and take any number of fresh pictures from a range of angles. Humour is a trick or trigger to free up the mind so that your thinking becomes less 'stuck'.

Seeing the familiar in a fresh light. Two approaches work here.

First, look at the meaning of concepts or words you are using to think about a problem and redefine them.

Let's take the word 'retirement'. A friend, aged 40, not particularly well-off, surprised those who knew him by saying that he had re-thought his life and decided to 'retire'. He had redefined the word as meaning that from now on he would only take on work that he loved doing. His career has thrived and, most importantly, he's more fulfilled.

Re-thinking work–life balance

In a similar vein, we could think afresh about the popular phrase work–life balance. The danger with this idea is that *it encourages us to think that work is somehow not life*: it's far more useful to think how we can put more 'life' into our work and let the idea of 'balance' go hang. The most fulfilled people I know are those who have dissolved the boundaries between work, love and play.

The creative use of *metaphor* is another way to see the old in new ways. You definitely need a sense of humour to use this effectively, as well as the ability to suspend disbelief.

Let's imagine you are working on the problem of how to find more time for your creative passions. You might start by thinking of the issue in metaphorical terms such as:

- A journey
- Space exploration
- Recording a song
- Gardening
- Training a dog

To work well you need to explore the parallel, metaphorical world thoroughly. This is Step 1 as shown in the diagram on p. 166. Let's suppose you've chosen 'recording a song'. The kinds of question that come to mind are:

- Are you better live or in the studio?
- How much rehearsal is needed?
- Should you go electric or do it 'unplugged'?
- What level of perfection are you aiming for? (First take or endless re-mastering?)
- Is it just a cover version or an original?
- What kind of a setting or studio would you use?
- What role are you playing: producer, vocalist, drummer, etc.?

In Step 1 you are deliberately not trying to make any conscious connections to the real problem of carving out more time for your creativity. Play with the parallel, metaphoric world long enough to let you stand back from the original problem that you were probably too close to. *Then* return (Step 2) to the real issue *using the language of the metaphysical world.*

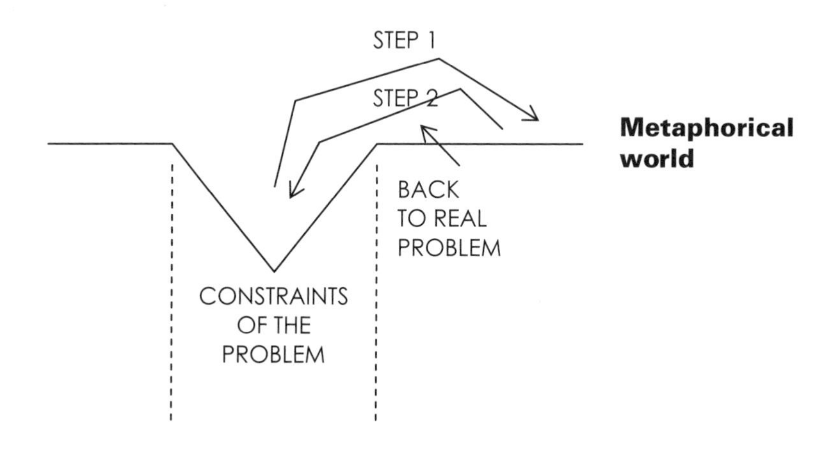

To relate this back to the problem of finding more time for your creative passions, this is exactly one I have had to address myself. Using the musical metaphor above opened a rich vein of thought.

Typically I'm a 'live band', giving many performances around the world, and find it hard to make time to 'go into the studio' to record, in other words write, make videos, etc. I've translated the metaphor from thin air into bricks and mortar by actually building a 'studio' where I can be at my most creative. Making it an appealing place to be is the only way I've resisted the urge to accept speaking engagements in exciting places like Bali, San Francisco or Iran.

But you may find any of the other questions insightful, for instance, the notion of a 'first take' or 'endless re-mastering'. Many people don't get down to their own form of creative work because they are waiting for the kids to leave home, for work to be less time-consuming, or for that elusive Lottery win. Waiting for Godot, in other words! In music, the 'first take' is uncannily often the one that works. Dylan's *Like A Rolling Stone* is an obvious example: not only was the released version the first try, but the accompanying musicians had never even heard the second half of the song and had no idea how it would end.

Try a 'first take'

Why not sit down today and attempt a *first take* at whatever idea has been on your mind – an article, a much mulled-over letter to a loved one, a watercolour, a first guitar lesson? There's magic in the first attempt!

By now I hope you've got the idea, so I'll deal with the last three types of humour more briefly.

Insight through humour means looking for the truth that a wry, elliptical view of the world throws up. In practice, it can mean perceiving the value in what appear to be throwaway lines.

For example, some years ago it was fashionable for organizations to introduce 'quality circles' to discuss and improve quality. The project a colleague and I were working on seemed to be losing its creative edge. During a meeting he mused, 'I'm fed up with quality circles. What about quality *squares*!?'

'That's it!' said the client. 'Add the customer in and that makes a square with the other three interest groups.' We did, and it worked. Not a new idea today, but it was at the time. Many a true word … Of course, humour can sometimes help us cope. As in writer Tony Parsons' observation that, 'Hell hath no fury like an ex-wife turned to fat'.

Surrealism is all about bizarre connections and combinations, and placing them in unusual contexts. What two or three elements of your problem can you juxtapose in an unusual way to create something new? In technology, Apple's use of artists, musicians and history graduates on product development teams adds a new aesthetic to design. In music, the Pet Shop Boys' combination of a lush techno sound with the vocal skills of chanteuse Dusty Springfield was surprisingly effective. And in business the homespun and funny labels on Innocent Smoothies make you take notice. I particularly like this advertisement:

'If you've enjoyed your Smoothie, why not try our other products like sand, rainbows, or perhaps plankton.'

Humour captures the notion of naturalness far better than a list of healthy ingredients.

A game you can play to exercise your surrealist mode is one I enjoyed with school friends. It's called 'Juxtapose', or 'Just suppose'. Practise creating combinations in pub naming, for example.

The Mole and Compasses sounds fine, as does the Plug And Bison, but somehow the Cock and Camel or the Rat And Parrot don't quite work (and these are real ones!). So not all juxtapositions are useful – the challenge is to make the elements so tangentially related that they create a frisson of surprise. As in the real London pub name, the Frog and Nightgown.

You can extend this play to juxtaposing people, concepts, environments and objects that wouldn't be natural bedfellows. Just suppose …

Making you use your imagination. The parrot joke ('The others call him the Master!') leaves you with a number of unanswered but startling questions. What *can* he do? How do the other parrots know this? How do they really regard him? And so on.

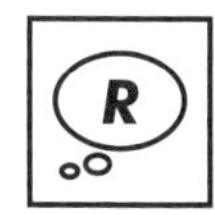

Similarly, it's a valuable technique in re-thinking to pose unusual questions that stretch the mind and force you to use your imagination. These are best framed as 'what ifs'.

'What if I were to cancel this project?'

'What if I were to start again from the beginning – what would I change?'

'What if I were to do nothing?'

Take the ideas that emerge, however ludicrous to your rational mind, for a long walk. You are actually creating a new chemistry in your brain, walking on the roads less travelled. Thinking will always be the fastest way to travel.

Just for the joy of it

Expressed logically like this you can miss the lateral, tangential value of humour in re-imagining a problem; a superfluid kind of thought that escapes from any analytical container you try to put it in. Above all, humour is a way of relaxing the narrowly focused mind to allow intuition to come to the forefront. In other words, it's not just a problem-solving technique but a different state of brain, emotion and physiology that is health-giving.

Play has its own value, and doesn't need to be justified as a utilitarian adjunct to the more important business of work. Recent research shows that songbirds sing far longer than the practical call of finding a mate or marking territory accounts for. The very non-scientific conclusion that they may be singing just for the joy of it shouldn't escape us.

Much laughter and humour is similarly just for the joy of it, even though when we think about it more coolly we can attach practical benefits. A very analytical friend benefited greatly from treatments in the Indian natural health system of Ayurveda. Apart from lifestyle and dietary recommendations, he received one piece of advice that made anyone who knew this serious man laugh out loud at its appropriateness. He was simply told: 'Read more comics!'

Here's the tricky part: if you think this advice is trivial or silly you may be the kind of person who needs to adopt it the most.

Try reading ...

... I can't resist suggesting *Puckoon* by Spike Milligan, *The Third Policeman* by Flann O'Brien, *The Blandings Castle* novels by P.G. Wodehouse or *Dirk Gently's Holistic Detective Agency* by Douglas Adams. Or, failing that, just try more comics!

re-think seven

Simply beautiful

Beauty does not come up very often in conversation. When it does, three things are often said about it. First, it's in the eye of the beholder. Then someone may mention Keats' lines about beauty being truth, and finally there's talk about the best scientific or artistic solutions having a kind of beauty to them.

Now this sounds like a fairly intellectual discussion, doesn't it? The problem is that it rarely gets going because the first observation scotches much further exploration. 'It's all relative, isn't it?' is the phrase that stops the conversation in its tracks. Philosophically, this is a valid position. It's called relativism.

While this view does contain truth, it's a dead end because it believes any notion of one thing being intrinsically more beautiful than another is a form of intellectual fascism. Either/or thinking has triumphed: *either* there's an absolute standard of beauty that constrains the emergence of new forms, *or* there's a relativistic free for all in which anything goes. There must be room for a re-think.

Ugliness in thinking

Let's start with the absence of beauty – ugliness. I want to begin with thinking because this is where ugliness in politics, architecture, the environment or the arts stems from. By ugly thoughts I don't just mean ones confined to aggression, violence or the need to shock in order to destroy old structures. I mean the thinking that comes from the more superficial, transient *level* of existence. The surface of the ocean of our consciousness rather than its silent depths. Ugliness is transitory, disposable, functional for a limited time.

Beauty, in contrast, has more of the timeless and the eternal about it, rarely pushes itself in your face, but requires an appreciation to dawn in you. For you to come to it. Blake's famous lines on perception are a recognition of this, as well as clearly describing a different state of being where the finite and the infinite co-exist:

To see a world in a grain of sand
And a heaven in a wild flower
Hold infinity in the palm of your hand
And eternity in an hour.[1]

His insight comes from a more beautiful level of the mind, beautiful in that it perceives *both* surface values *and* timelessness. But if the doors of our perception are closed, then relativism becomes the fixed dogma. As it has today.

Ugliness in thinking is also enshrined in our way of life through what writer and thinker Edward de Bono describes as a poor understanding of the legacy of Greek thinkers. He calls Socrates, Plato and Aristotle the 'Gang of Three'. What have these thinkers got to do with you and I? Quite a lot. The notion of putting forward a *thesis*, which is then confronted by an *antithesis,* and followed by constructive *synthesis,* appears in a bastardized form in our political, legal and educational systems, and the very way in which we conduct everyday conversations.

---

1 William Blake, *Auguries of Innocence* (c. 1803).

So, in Parliament we hear one member say (thesis), 'Does not the Right Honourable Member for Penge think that he has been a fool/corrupt/reckless/ill-advised/lying (delete as appropriate), and should resign forthwith?'

I don't think I need to reply for the honourable member; he's in the blue corner, his opponent's in the red corner, and they'll slug it out until truth leaves the building. This is why when governments use the expression, 'Let's have a public *debate* on this matter', our hearts sink as we know that we're unlikely to see a synthesis any time soon. Debate rarely progresses beyond thesis/antithesis, and although this has the noble aim of one party being able to test another's thesis and not take it at face value, the usual effect is to leave each side more deeply entrenched in their original position.

It's this ugliness in thought, identification with the more superficial and divisive levels of the mind, that's brought ugliness into the way our religions and democracies have begun to behave in the world despite the wonderful ideals of their founders. Lop-sided, partial thinking is opposed to the connected, more whole styles of being that welcome the co-existence of opposites, in race, belief systems, religions and ways of life. Thought precedes action, and it doesn't take long for *my* thesis to become a bomb and your *antithesis* to become bombers.

You are what you see

If you see ugliness around you, you will tend to behave in an uglier way. Several studies have shown that if you put people, even educated teenagers, in a shabby environment, they will tend to take on the attributes of their surroundings, in some cases trashing it even further. But surround them with beauty and there's a tendency to preserve it and to feel more at ease in themselves.

Child psychologist Bruno Bettleheim ran the Orthogenic School at the University of Chicago for emotionally disturbed children. Beauty was the touchstone for everything that surrounded these children, as extreme as having gold leaf on the doorways and flowers in every room.

The immediate objection to this line of thinking is obvious: we can't all live in palaces (and many a bloody dictator has lived in beautiful surroundings). Outer beauty alone does not guarantee inner harmony.

But in our everyday lives, we do have the opportunity to seek out, choose and enjoy the beautiful more than we realize. Unless we have the luxury of an income that allows us to furnish our home with Impressionist paintings and Ming vases, we're just going to have to be a little more creative about it ...

Think first of the notion that 'you are what you see'. The more familiar saying is that 'you are what you eat': in the same way this has made us increasingly conscious about taking less toxic matter into our bodies, we need to become more careful of what we take in visually and through our senses generally.

Let's start with the news, which I don't believe should be censored, but *self*-censored. If some terrible atrocity occurs, does it help to watch the scene replayed again and again and again? To hear 15 eyewitness accounts of the incident, followed by hours of time-filling by 'expert' commentators?

It's ironic that the same newscaster can say terrorists are homicidal maniacs (they are) and also publicity-seekers for their cause, and then give them 24 hours of total news coverage. Too much horror and we shut down. We are not inspired to act, but freeze like the proverbial rabbit in the headlights. That's why I prefer to hear news on the radio, and am partial to Dylan's line, 'I prefer old news'.

We should balance our daily intake of information and ideas to take in real nourishment. What's good for the individual soul is also good for the world.

Beautiful *and* useful

This brings us, perhaps inevitably, to William Morris's comment that we should only have what's useful and what we *believe* to be beautiful in our homes. Look around you: can you say that? While so many are aspiring to acquire more possessions, the problem in the first world is that of being cluttered with too much, too many machines that need maintenance, too many unwanted gifts that crowd our homes. We now have television programmes that denounce hoarding as an addiction (it is), and offer to help us throw stuff out to 'de-clutter' our lives. There are even consultants that will help you in these seemingly straightforward tasks. We should do it for ourselves.

You may say on your CV that you like literature or poetry, but when was the last time you really sat down and read something that moved and uplifted you? Or read poems aloud as they were intended, either to yourself or with a group of friends? Poet and speaker David Whyte introduces serious business groups to the idea of reading a poem a day. He advises that :

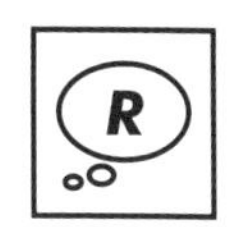

'You could do worse than read a Robert Frost poem each day.' Or when did you sit down last to hear all of, say, the St Matthew Passion at one hearing, uninterrupted by mobile calls or the television?

The same is true with the visual arts. I like to use a projector to show a different slide of a great painting on my white living room wall every week or, if I'm feeling more speedy, every day. I know it's not the same impact as the original, but it certainly rests and comforts my eyes to see a Poussin or Fra Angelico in the morning and when I come home from work.

This is more like William Blake's notion of art, that it shouldn't be something we go to a gallery to see, but should surround us and enrich our everyday perceptions. After all, here's a man who saw angels in a tree on Peckham Rye, now a busy and crowded area of south London.

To find what's beautiful, you may need to enlist the help of an enthusiast: tuning into another's view of beauty is one of the greatest benefits of being curious, a seeker of the new.

We are often too busy trying to communicate what we find inspiring to others. Switch on to 'receive mode' and you will find the range of beauty open to you greatly expanded. I've done this with opera, art, poetry and music. I don't always agree with my friends' views, but in the process I've come across some passions that would never have been open to me.

John Lane observes in his profound book *Timeless Beauty*[2] that beauty is an unfashionable subject and perhaps the word itself is too effete to really convey its impact on our sensibilities. This is because in our age of relativism, even proposing that there is a hierarchy in beauty is seen as old school, restrictive thinking. To say that Raphael is better than Bacon or even that the Beatles' music is more rich than that of the Strokes is regarded as backward-looking, fogeyish and authoritarian. When we start comparing our views of beauty, we quickly get hot under the collar: we're no longer appreciating, but criticizing and comparing.

So let's partially accept the relative view that if someone finds something beautiful, then that is real to them. But while it's possible to get the juice out of even the skin of an orange, it's just much harder work. I can hear *glimpses* of beauty in Eminem's music, but I can see whole vistas in John Coltrane's.

---

[2] John Lane, *Timeless Beauty*, Green Books, 2003.

Natural beauty

Of course, much art is not produced with the aim of conveying beauty: it's to shock, express an emotion, break a taboo, or overthrow the old order. Its modern expression is in ironic music, disposable art, computer-generated images and so on. This is not all bad; if the Renaissance was still here, the subject matter for painting might still be restricted to the religious and historical. The drive to include the mundane within the reach of the arts, to say that no subject material is out of bounds, is why we see toilet fittings and works made out of elephant dung in our major galleries. We should not be comparing this with older, often rigid views of 'what art is', but instead thinking how this makes us feel, to what extent does this arouse a sense of beauty within us?

A richer seam of beauty is found when a building, an object, a sculpture or a poem approaches timelessness. When it refines your perceptions, giving you a taste of bliss more than a buzz of excitement, and when it allows you to feel connected to the more beautiful – and truthful – aspects of your own nature.

The laws that exist in nature need to be, and I believe will be, adopted more into manmade artefacts and art. Natural law is not a restriction in the same way as manmade law, but rather a form of harmonious liberation because of the almost infinite diversity of the physical universe. The concept of 'higher' art may lead to snobbery when its arbiters are professional art critics, a kind of beauty police. But if we think of 'higher' as that which draws us closer to the eternal and timeless, then we are on the right track.

The Fibonacci sequence is a wonderful example of timeless beauty in nature. It was discovered by the monk Leonardo of Pisa, nicknamed Fibonacci. He came across a significant sequence of numbers: 1, 1, 2, 3, 5, 8, 13, 21, 34, 55, 89, 144 and so on, where each new number is created by adding together the two previous numbers. This sequence is exhibited in many forms in Nature: seed displays, on pineapples, the spirals of snail shells and, most strikingly, in the head of an ordinary sunflower.

John Lane describes the extraordinary mathematics of Nature in the spirals of the sunflower, where there is one set of spirals going clockwise and another anti-clockwise from the centre.

> *These two sinuous spirals reveal the astonishing double connection with the Fibonacci series:*
>
> *The pairs are always adjacent numbers in the Fibonacci series, e.g. one pair could be 21 and 34 and the next pair could be 34 and 55.*
>
> *The adjacent numbers divided yield the Golden Section, 34/55 = 0.618 or 54/34 = 1.618.*

Unveiling the mathematical beauty of Nature reminds us that 'invention' is finding what is already there. The Golden Section, which exists as a set of natural proportions in the human body, was used in the design of temples like the Parthenon. In this deepest sense we can think of the search for beauty as a creative journey that unveils timeless truths about our world. Beauty as truth, truth as beauty.

Lane has a wonderful re-think on this point, suggesting we should not look at Nature as the artist's inspiration, but at Nature as the artist.

The Parthenon may seem far from an inner-city tenement, but more creative principles can be applied even to lower-cost housing. In Vienna, the eccentric artist Hunterwasser was asked to design inner-city housing and produced wondrous buildings that look as if they came out of a fairy tale. In England, a house in Norfolk designed to ancient Vedic principles recently won a major 'eco-house' award. In America, hundreds of dwellings from homes to office blocks have recently been built conforming to this ancient idea of correct Vastu, a tradition that pre-dates Feng Shui.

Vastu is based on correct orientation, siting, materials and proportion. 'Correct' not according to any faddish architectural canon, but in the sense of being aligned with natural laws such as the rising and setting of the sun.

Buildings affect us. The theory is that if a building defies certain natural principles, it will have an adverse effect on us. 'Sick-building disease' is not psychosomatic – we know from experience that certain environments affect us physically in negative ways, and even hinder our ability to think clearly. Initial research is indicating that the neurons in our brain are affected by our physical surroundings and even fire in different ways according to our orientation to the sun. All of this is taken into account in the Vastu[3] design. You feel well in these buildings, and your mind works better.

If this seems far-fetched, just look around you. Houses being hurriedly assembled today too often look like Lego because their design is driven by functionality and economics. When windows are misplaced, as they often are, our innate sense of aesthetics is affronted. Principles like the Golden Mean – proportions which are intrinsically pleasing to the eye and soul as they are founded on the same laws with which the most beautiful entity in the world, the human body, is designed – need to be rediscovered, albeit with modern materials and building techniques.

It's often said that windows are the eyes of a house, which is a strong metaphor for the uncaring, lop-sided way we look out at our relationship to the environment. A more harmonious inner sense of beauty is the first step to start reducing the ugliness we see around us.

---

[3] Originally from the Vedic tradition of 'Sthapatya Veda' from India, meaning 'to establish'.

Beautiful solutions

Scientists often talk about 'beautiful solutions'. Einstein was as much an artist as a scientist. The search for knowledge is the search for beauty, as discovered in the 'enchanted loom' of our brains and the double-helix of our DNA.

'So beautiful!' is how scientist John Schwarz describes mathematical structures of the most leading modern physics, string theory. Physicist Paul Dirac even argued that beauty should be the first criterion to look for in coming up with new theoretical models. It's remarkable that Keats' linking of beauty to truth, often dismissed as poetical whimsy, is finding a new life in the breakthroughs of empirical science.

A more beautiful solution tends to come from more settled and expanded – we could even say more beautiful – levels of the mind. This is accessed most easily through meditation, quiet reflection or periods of solitude. We can link the concept of beauty to everyday themes by realizing that it means more:

Elegance – Is there grace in your solution?

Simplicity – What 'clutter' can you eliminate to make your idea simpler?

Naturalness – Is there artifice blocking the directness of your thinking?

Pleasure – What's the emotional impact of your idea?

Grace in the air

As a frequent air traveller, it's clear to me that a sense of beauty in the art of service is often ignored. Compare the clunkiness of delivery – say, on British Airways – with the grace of a Singapore Airlines stewardess. Both fly similar airplanes under similar conditions. But the difference is day and night.

In service industries a major re-think would be to train all staff in the beauty and grace of performing the smallest acts, such as serving a cup of coffee.

These are criteria we can apply to obvious situations such as laying a table for guests, or just for you and your partner. One experience of a genuine Chinese or Japanese tea ceremony, and I can't help regretting the absence of ritual in the West, and feeling somewhat gross in the routine of slurping tea from a mug. Or worse, the awful containers that beverages from catering machines arrive in. 'Catering' is a concept that should be banned because it nearly always implies the most cost-efficient 'delivery of a solution'. Even the language is ugly!

A writer from India observed how in England people drink awful tea from plastic cups. He wrote to his family describing how poor we were over here. 'They can't even afford proper cups,' he said. He is not talking about poor in the sense of poverty, but rather the *impoverishment* of a life diminished by a lack of beauty in its small everyday rituals.

But there's no reason why elegance, simplicity, naturalness and an aesthetic of what's pleasing should not be applied to everyday activities such as answering the telephone, crafting an email or presenting a message to others. Or in daily routines such as welcoming a guest or serving a meal.

You are *how* you eat

It's fashionable for TV chefs to swear in the kitchen. My experience is that someone's state of mind when they cook finds its way into the food.

The conditions in which you eat can also cause your digestive system to relax or rebel. If you find yourself standing up to cram in a sandwich, you know which it will be.

Try at least once a week having a meal in silence, appreciate it through every sense before eating, and have your attention on the process of eating and nothing else. We can think of eating as just absorbing the fuel we need, or as taking in parcels of intelligence from the environment. You choose.

When you eat is also insufficiently thought about. Want to lose weight? *Having a cooked meal at lunchtime and then something very light in the evening will make more difference than all but the most extreme diets you can go on.* This would be a *major* re-think in our working day!

If you're working on something more complex, such as creating a new home or even building one, beauty should be as much of a consideration as function. Indeed, if you get it right, the two should merge. My emphasis on discovering or unveiling beauty in natural forms doesn't mean we can't re-think and produce something new that marries elegance and effectiveness. I've been somewhat sceptical when people say that a piece of technology is beautiful, but I was converted by my iPod. It certainly wins out over other MP3 players in elegance and simplicity, as well as the intuitive way it operates. Being able to control it by feel in the dark is a triumph of design, which helps me to forgive its practical defects such as poor battery life and a tendency to jog tracks while moving. This level of focus on beautiful *design* will be the hallmark of successful products – even mass-market ones – in the future. Look forward to the return of beauty.

RE-THINK NO. 16: SURROUND YOURSELF WITH BEAUTY

Beauty is an inner as well as an outer concept.

Outwardly, we can and should 'do a William Morris' and make sure that we are physically surrounded by objects and artefacts of beauty, whether your preferred style is minimalist or chintzy. The truth in 'you are what you see' means our eyes should alight as much as possible on uplifting images.

It can be a simple vase of flowers, a great quotation, or whatever fires your creative imagination. In particular, the black boxes and hard lines of technology in our homes – TVs, music systems, fridges, etc. – should be softened by the natural beauty of plants. This is not mere aesthetics: when objects are 'inanimate' it means they are not possessing *anima* or mind, whereas being in natural beauty means we are touched by the anima or soul of living things. Jung observed that 'sometimes a tree tells you more than can be read in books.'

Beauty in solitude

'In solitude, we give passionate attention to our lives, to our memories, to the details around us.'

Virginia Woolf

But if the inner is the basis of the outer, we should also be concerned with the beauty, or lack of it, that we absorb into our minds. Relativism has its place, but we should not be sucked into the current fashion for believing that one thing is as valuable as any other; that there is no hierarchy in beauty.

The hierarchy should not be prescribed by others, but based upon what is more timeless. This is closer to Plato's vision of transcendent forms – that creativity unveils or discovers as much as it makes. In this sense, 'surrounding yourself with beauty' means a search for ideas, music and sights that put you more in touch with the truth that's inherent in beauty.

The key is firstly to accept that what goes into our mind and eyes is as powerful an influence as the food we eat. Otherwise we are prey to the superstition of materialism, that what appears to be more solid and real – our physical body – is somehow more important than mind and emotion.

Next is the realization that we do have *choice* as to what we allow into our minds. This is actually more difficult than it sounds, as there are many with a vested interest in ensuring that we have no choice but to hear *their* message: advertisers, broadcasters, news merchants, all shouting loudly to grab a part of our minds. It's even called 'share of attention' by marketers. No wonder silence and solitude are two of the great scarcities in the twenty-first century.

Let's take the notion of what you allow to flower in your mind, which Oxford scientist Kathleen Taylor calls 'cultivating our synaptic garden'. She's describing the spaces between the neurons of the brain that hold the beliefs and perceptions that condition us to respond in specific ways. This wonderful image of a mental 'garden' encourages us to escape from brainwashing and create a new fertile soil for fresh perceptions in our own mind.

Ways of cultivating our inner garden include:

- *Spending more time with the most positive, uplifting people (or failing that, those with a wry wit and interesting perceptions).*
- *Seeing the highest or most beautiful qualities in other people.*
- *Stopping to admire beauty more often – finding a rhythm that's not clock time.*
- *Being more in nature – find your beautiful spots and visit them more often.*
- *Choosing timelessness over transience.*
- *Finding beauty in small rituals – from morning coffee to the way we communicate with friends and family.*
- *Using beauty as the measuring stick for any possessions we acquire.*
- *Always searching for a more elegant or beautiful solution.*

More than anything, there's beauty in thinking for ourselves, and not accepting mediocrity or someone else's standards. The thinking error that allows us to be surrounded with too much ugliness is that the average is somehow normal. Accept this, and you may stop searching for more beauty, which is ultimately more truth.

re-think | eight

Storytime!

Stories produce change better than dry abstractions. If you were told to be kind to others, would it have as much of an impact as the Biblical tale of the kind Samaritan who crosses the road to help an ailing person? I doubt it, because in the latter case you can see in your mind's eye the *act* of crossing the street: it evokes a more potent and visceral response. Stories are more practical than cool injunctions.

We are all unconsciously influenced by the stories we are told, read and hear, especially in our earlier, more impressionable days. Most of us experience real life as more Grimm Brothers than Disney. Although Hollywood operates well at the level of entertainment, it's less effective in preparing us for the real witches, wizards and spells we encounter in life.

The psychologist Bruno Bettelheim researched over two decades the effects on children of being read sanitized fairy stories with the nasty bits removed. Many of our original tales and myths have some fairly x-rated sequences. He claims that these children grew up as adults less equipped to handle the hurly burly of adult life.

What is clear is that stories – from moral tales to our great religious teachings – influence us in a deeper way than we are consciously aware.

Despite attempts in our rational age to sideline them as pure escapism, fantasy or entertainment there has been a huge revival in storytelling in the last decade. Storytelling groups reviving the old tales have sprung up in nearly all Western countries. Perhaps a *cri de coeur* for the absence of meaning in society, divorced from our older stories by globalization, standardization and the ascendancy of technology.

Story's deeper purpose

It's clear that the need for stories transcends our desire for entertainment, although this is not to disparage the value of a great yarn. *The Lord of the Rings*, conceived as pure story by its author J R R Tolkien, consistently wins polls of readers' favourite book of all time.

But in some societies storytelling is perceived as the thread that gives knowledge, identity and a sense of purpose, almost as important to life as bread itself. This is particularly true of the African oral tradition of storytelling. While some might consider stories as being akin to superstitions that need to be swept away, Kenyan Nobel Prizewinner Wangari Maathai has quite another view.

She argues with passion and insight how her country's threatened ecology and disappearing biological diversity can only be solved if there's a revival of Kenya's cultural heritage, one based on the old stories. Mount Kenya is a powerful example. From this mountain flows many of the country's rivers, but a combination of irresponsible logging, monoculture and climate change has threatened the environment. Mount Kenya used to be perceived by the Kikuyus as the abode of God. This God would ensure that everything good flowed to them, including clean water and rains.

The missionaries had another story to impose, telling the Kikuyu that God did not dwell in Mount Kenya but in heaven. Wangari Maathai says:

> *'Heaven is not above us: it is right here, right now. So the Kikuyu people were not wrong when they said that God dwelled on the mountain because if God is omnipresent, as theology tells us, then God is on Mount Kenya too. If believing that God is on Mount Kenya is what helps people conserve their mountain, I say that's OK. If people still believed this, they would not have allowed illegal logging or clear-cutting of the forest.'*[1]

Here, the so-called primitive language of the indigenous people – contrasting with the First World's description of itself as 'civilized' – is more pragmatic and a more accurate reflection of the original teachings of Christianity. God's omnipresence – indeed the creator's role as manifester of the world's diversity – seems to have been conveniently forgotten in a desire to impose a particularly narrow story of religion on people who held their own beliefs for centuries.

Maathai's point is profound: reviving cultures and the stories that sustain them might be the *only* thing that can prevent destruction of the environment. Planting trees without the understanding of the 'why' behind the action is a lost cause.

Without rediscovering our own cultural 'story' and how the adventure of our own life fits into that bigger story, we all lose our way and sense of identity. It's happened in the UK in the same way it's happened in Africa. For us, losing our unique stories and having to live out a life ruled by the ogre of productivity leads to stressful working practices, having money but no time to enjoy life.

---

[1] 'The Cracked Mirror', Wangari Maathai, *Resurgence*, pp. 21–3, November/December 2004, No. 227.

The need for stories

'Tell them stories. That's what we didn't know. All this time, and we never knew! But they need the truth. That's what nourishes them. You must tell them true stories, and everything will be well, everything. Just tell them stories.'

Philip Pullman, *The Amber Spyglass*

Stories convey beliefs and underpin the values that drive our behaviour. But what has this got to do with re-thinking?

Let's start with the use of story as a metaphor, and explore the kind of myth you might unwittingly be living out. Is your life a comedy, a farce, a tragedy, or a mixture of all three? Do you feel you have been set a series of impossible labours like the ones that faced Heracles, but unfortunately are not equipped with his staying power and keep failing on the ultimate challenge, for instance, getting on with your ex-spouse? Or are you fortunate enough to feel you have an angelic fairy godmother smiling on you, and wish she would also stick around to help you with your tax returns?

Now the glib self-help advice would be to tell you to step out of any story you're not enjoying and to write a new script! Sadly it's not that easy, as poignantly captured by Peter Sellers' character Chauncey Gardiner in the film *Being There*. Evicted from his nest, he's left with only a TV remote control, and when he meets with threatening muggers in the street his impulse is to point the remote at them to change the channel to a more palatable programme. This is like being told to 'choose a new attitude': it doesn't happen by pressing a button.

More than metaphor

A story gives us a vibrant and rich framework within which to re-think our life's passage, much in the same way that the Samaritan's tale is more compelling than a theoretical commandment to 'do good'. Stories are hard-wired into us: they tap into ways of intuitively understanding the subtle currents that flow through our lives. They take a very similar form through all cultures throughout recorded time because they embody essential truths about the adventure of human life. Whatever is nearer to the truth, lasts.

This is wonderfully encapsulated in mythology expert Joseph Campbell's famous lines:

> *'The latest incarnation of Oedipus, the continued romance of Beauty and the Beast, stand this afternoon on the corner of 42nd Street and Fifth Avenue, waiting for the traffic light to change.'*

Let's take some simple characters: Jack the Giant Slayer (the little man who overcomes gigantic odds), the Princess who needs to be rescued (brilliantly parodied in the film *Shrek*), and the Little Mermaid (who exemplifies the pain of unrequited love). It's worth considering which of these you identify with and why. Two contrasting destinies face the Little Tailor and the Cobbler. The Little Tailor seems unencumbered by worldly responsibilities, stepping out into bright sunshine to make his fortune and in the process outwitting giants who have slain many stronger foes. He's Ulysses-lite, but compelling nonetheless.

In contrast, the Cobbler always struggles to make ends meet and however hard he works seems unable to shoe his own children (for 'shoe' read private school education or the latest trainers). It's the fate of the workaholic who never has time to enjoy the fruits of his labour.

Which do you identify with right now? If we think of our life as a story and believe there's something of the hero or heroine in us, then that's the part of our nature we need to activate to break out of a tale that's not going our way. This is real magic, the realization that life doesn't have to be something that happens to us while we're busy making other plans. It's waking up from the spell that's been weaved over us, the spell that blinds us to how much we can become the author of our own story.

Writing your own future

There's a task that's often given in self-development seminars or even in job interviews. You have to write your own obituary or, in the short version, the inscription you would like to see on your gravestone. (*Practical tip* – just write 'I made a difference' and you'll pass. Or if they're looking for humour try using comedian Spike Milligan's version: 'I told you I was ill.')

It's difficult to imagine the future. A work by the famous British artist Damien Hirst is entitled *The Impossibility of Death in the Mind of Someone Living,* which neatly gives us the size of the problem. When I get people to write their own individual story, I suggest a timeframe of one to two years from today. It's just about conceivable and gives you enough appetite for the goal to get working on it.

The first step is to write a *before* and *after* story. The Before stage describes a day in your life now; the After describes a more desirable future. I'm using the notion of story in a very simplified form, meaning a narrative with a protagonist and a journey. You'll see shortly why this is a more effective method than writing down a list of goals. These, like New Year's resolutions, so often lack animation, lie flat on the page, and simply don't work as well.

Here's an example from someone I coached (true story, but name changed).

Frank's story: Before

Frank Wilkinson is a 43-year-old marketing executive with a software company based in Maidenhead, England.

> *I wake up at 6 a.m. – 45 minutes before the alarm's due to go off. Or rather, I'm woken up by Jason playing noisily with his Star Wars toys and arguing loudly with Emma. I hardly feel as if I've slept, and there's a deep dread about the 1½ hours' drive to work, including a 40-minute detour in nearly stationary traffic to get Emma to private school.*
>
> *Jane (my wife) tells me as I'm getting dressed that we still haven't done the re-mortgaging forms, and have I remembered we're having dinner at the Randalls' tonight. Instead of doing the run I promised myself last night as I slumped in front of Big Brother I found myself refereeing a fight between the kids and trying to focus on the incomprehensible bank paperwork while my coffee went cold. Out of the door, but just as I'm starting off I remember the PowerPoint presentation for the ad team that I've left on my desktop in the spare room. Ten minutes later, with Emma fretting about being late for school (again), I'm in the car, realizing I haven't kissed Jane goodbye.*
>
> *I get to work – half an hour late – and my secretary tells me I've already got four calls and six urgent emails, including one from a client I should have responded to last night.*
>
> *All day long I realize I'm rushing and lunch is just a sandwich at the desk as I try to restore some order to my day. I'm called into two crisis meetings and the boss interrupts me three times as I try to finish my presentation for the Institute of Marketing I'm due to deliver tomorrow. I stay late to try to finish it. It takes ages longer than I planned because of unexpected phone calls. Then*

> *I remember the Randalls, race out to the car park without my presentation, run back again to get it, and then find myself stuck on the M25 with the late leavers.*
>
> *Arriving at home hassled and frustrated, I find Jane giving me the cold shoulder as I've got five minutes to change before we go out to a dinner date I don't want to go to. I spend most of the five minutes changing and briefing and paying the babysitter, leaving me no time to say a proper goodnight to Jason and Emma.*
>
> *As I go to sleep I'm still thinking about that unfinished presentation, and resolve to get up earlier, knowing in my heart of hearts that I won't.*

Clearly there's a lot that needs changing or re-thinking in Frank's life. You and I of course have the benefit of a bird's-eye view and can easily muscle in with some helpful feedback or advice. The advantage of writing today's story is that you gain an outsider's fly-on-the-wall view of your own life, warts and all. Much of the advice we could give Frank he could probably give to himself, but his internal conversation would probably be clouded by a great deal of 'yes, butting' the changes he knows he needs to make. Oscar Wilde has an expression for this (he usually does):

> *'I always pass on good advice. It is the only thing to do with it. It is never of any use to oneself.'*[2]

So instead of giving advice to Frank, I got him to give it to himself, firstly by writing down the elements of the life he wanted to be living in a year's time, and then weaving it into the day in the life story that follows.

---

[2] From *An Ideal Husband*, 1895.

Frank's story: The future

It's 7.30 a.m. and I'm packing my son and daughter into the car for the school run. Many parents find this a stressful time: not me! It's a chance to share everyday hopes and concerns on the 15-minute journey, not just to indulge in quality time that can become so unreal and frenetic. I'm so glad we decided to move them out of that academically 'excellent' but one-hour-away establishment. The sense of community we all share with their friends and other parents is so much more rewarding.

It's also been good for Jane, my wife. She's less of a taxi driver, more her own person. She's re-started her job – part-time of course – as producer at the local radio station. Freedom from school runs in the morning has made it possible for her to do the early morning show.

Dropping Emma and Jason off (they've forgotten X and Y as usual, but no panic), I've got another 20 minutes to get to work in the software company where I'm marketing director. Time to play my Japanese tape. OK, I've only learned the conversational (very) basics so far, but it's a real wow with clients when I'm over there. Also, it's given me real insight and fascination with their culture. Much better than being depressed by the radio news.

When I arrive in reception Debbie gives me a warm smile and welcome. That idea I put into practice about how we can make Z... 'A great place to work' has really rubbed off on most (though not all) of the people. There's a buzz and an energy around the building we just didn't have a year ago. It helps us through the grotty days, too.

I remember reading that book about time management, saying how you start the day is vital to making the rest of it go well. We start off with a 20-minute team meeting, and are never interrupted unless it's the boss, F…, with one of his rants!

Most of the team contribute to the meeting. I wouldn't say they are gung ho by the time they leave, but at least staying in touch like this means there's a sense of purpose during the day – and less big communication cock-ups. It had obviously been worth it to take them – partners and all – to that smart hotel in the country to thrash out our joint goals and sense of purpose.

The morning is the usual pressure: dozens of emails, a video conference and phone calls, but by 12.30 I put in half an hour of sweat in the small in-company gym we decided to put in, and enjoyed a cooked (if brief) lunch at the café down the road. All those resolutions I made about flattening my stomach are finally carrying through.

The afternoon is meetings, meetings, but the fact that I'm definitely leaving at 5.30 unless there's a real emergency keeps me focused. Also, there's the anticipation of my guitar lesson. This is one of those things I'd always meant to do, and I find a weekly session means I can at least start having a bash at those folk favourites (very basic versions!) two or three times a week at home. It's brought me much satisfaction, even though my 10-year-old laughed the first time she heard me straining at 'Scarborough Fair'.

Evening meals with the family are now a vital ritual in my life. My wife and I were appalled at the TV dinner, fragmented life that goes on in most homes, and eating en famille *is one of the good memories we both share from our own upbringing. When we first instituted it a year ago, the kids groaned, especially when we made rules like no Gameboys or TV watching. In fact, putting the TV in the playroom was one of the best decisions we made, as well as not answering the phone during dinner. Our teenager's still strong on grunts and evasion, but gradually we're learning as a family to have some kind of conversation that's a little more healthy than the Big Brother variety.*

After dinner Jane and I go for a walk and catch up on the day. It's one of the few times we're really alone together and find out what's going on with each other. We listen, make plans and try to keep the small stuff like bills, meetings, dinner dates and the rest to one side. We wrestle the kids away from the TV and PlayStation and spend some time reading amusing bits to each other from the day's papers. Ten minutes on the guitar and I'm ready for bed. It's not a red letter day, but it feels pretty perfect to me.

What's intriguing is that whenever I get individuals or teams to write their stories, the 'today' version usually oozes negativity. I haven't said write about your problems: just compress what's in your mind into a day. The value of this is therapeutic in allowing the person to step outside themselves long enough to get just a taste of objectivity. It's normally enough to make a huge difference, a practical way of applying the truth of 'out of sight, out of mind'. Using the mirror of the story, many of the writer's frustrations and dissatisfactions appear in sharper relief than before.

The assumption behind the future story is that it will be more positive, and strangely I've noticed that even people whose stance on life is normally pessimistic begin to see possibilities that they would censor as near impossible if you had asked them, for instance, to write a wish list about how they wanted their life to be. We still have a hunger for utopias, despite being bombarded by writers' and film-makers' obsession with dystopias.

A peculiar thing happens, a process familiar to most writers on a good day: once you *start* writing, *it's as if the story starts to write itself.* At first in fits and starts, and then with more of a sense of flow as initial scepticism that this is a crazy thing to do begins to fade. Ideas that you didn't have when you set out begin to seep in. My only instruction is to include them all in the first draft, letting them lead you where they will. The example you see is a much tidied-up version of Frank's first attempt, and some personal jokes and references have been edited out because, well, they're personal. Just as your story should be.

Nurturing your story

I can almost hear the objection in your mind. 'It's all very well to *write* the story, but what about the real world?' We all know about failed New Year's resolutions, so this is addressed in the re-think section.

Crafting the story is one thing, you will say, actually making the changes real quite another. I agree. But what I have experienced is something rather remarkable: just having the *intention* to take your life in this new direction makes your mind more open to the opportunities that come along, more receptive to the 'yes' in the environment. Although I grant you that without action the story will be mere fantasy, don't underestimate the power of 'seeing' your desired future laid out in this way.

I encourage all storywriters to both push out the boundaries and make their vision *achievable*. The distinction between advice that limits the writer and that which stops them being unrealistic is a fine one, but it's one that needs drawing. Are you likely to move from being a plumber to a Nobel Prizewinner in one year?

The main reason we read any story is to be able to find out what happens next. Frank's story turned out to be about 75 per cent (his own estimate) realized after a year. He did make the big change of moving the children's school, and his family life is significantly better. But as far as always leaving work at 5.30, he tells me he's only had partial success. Time to write another story?

Naturally, Frank's story is not nearly as interesting as your own, so dip into the practical instructions in the re-think section – and start! But one word of warning. Although you may eventually need to discuss your story with someone else – Frank's wouldn't have worked without comparing notes with his wife and children – be careful who you expose your story to, and when. The word 'expose' is carefully chosen here.

For your dreams to mature, they need a period of incubation. Leave them too long and mould gathers, but bring them out to the light too soon and somehow they become bleached out, weakened. And of course beware the dream-killers, those who haven't listened to Yeats' words:

'Tread softly for you tread on my dreams.'[3]

Let your ideas develop!

The brilliant pianist and composer André Tchaikovsky, made a great observation about his creative process. He said that if he was working on a new idea and shared it with someone too soon, it was like letting light into the film too early, preventing it from developing. This advice has been invaluable to me in many ways; when I hear myself mouthing off too quickly and to unreceptive people about a new idea, I sense with an inner groan of self-loathing that it's probably not going to happen!

A coda to this chapter comes from the mischievous wit of musician and composer André Tchaikovsky. It's an example of how you can write your story even beyond death. André held a lifelong ambition of being a Shakespearian actor, and had always wished to tread the boards at the

---

[3] W B Yeats, 'He Wishes for the Cloths of Heaven', 1899.

Royal Shakespeare Theatre in Stratford-on-Avon. In his will he made a bequest of his skull (the Home Office had to approve this) to the RSC. So perhaps next time Hamlet says, 'Alas, poor Yorick', André will, in a strange way, have achieved his aim.

Consider having a private version of your story, or start taking the first steps to manifest it before you show it to others. Re-thinking your life, even in the mundane details, is an intensely personal process of cultivating your inner state of mind to affect your outward behaviour. It's your life, your story.

RE-THINK NO. 17: WRITING AND LIVING YOUR STORY

The instructions, part I: Today's story

Find a quiet, private place and start. Make a note of the ingredients of your life – work, family, pleasure, self-development – as you see them today. Firstly, encapsulate your view of your life in a 'day in the life' story.

Some poetic licence is allowed as you will probably need to compress into 24 hours more than generally happens. This is fine. You are writing, in true Hollywood fashion, a story 'based on a true story'.

Most importantly, don't censor thoughts that come into your head. Put them in the first draft as it's usually easier to edit than expand. And remember that this is for your eyes only, at least at this time, so no censorship is required. This is more difficult than it seems, so the trick is just to *keep writing*! One or two pages is usually enough.

You now have a kind of mirror that allows you to stand back and look at yourself *in action* rather than as a frozen reflection or photograph. Pick it up and quietly reflect on it over the next day or two.

Ask yourself:

- *Do I recognize this person?*
- *What are the obvious changes or improvements I would like to make in the way I lead my life?*
- *Have I included enough about relationships with those dear to me?*
- *Am I leading the creative life I know I should be leading?*
- *Am I writing this story or does it seem as if the script is being written for me – by others, by circumstances?*

The last question is the most significant: how much you *believe* you can write your own future will be the most important factor in realizing it. As Henry Ford once remarked, 'If you believe you can, or believe you can't, you're probably right!'

Frank's story in the first part of this chapter was mainly negative at this 'before' stage. Is yours? If so, don't worry, as this is the grit in the oyster that can spur you on to change your story.

The instructions, part II: Story of the future

Now you can write the future as you desire it to be.

Not as a pipedream or in the hackneyed sense of writing your own obituary, but in an inspiring and achievable form. You choose the time-scale, but from my coaching experience I would suggest 6–18 months as realistic. No Stalinist five-year plans, or at least not for your first attempt.

Don't look at today's story. It's already in your mind and too much focus on it can pull you back into current difficulties.

Start with writing down the changes you desire. A useful checklist is:

- Self-development
- Fulfilment
- Job/career/achievements
- Relationships – friends and family
- Lifestyle
- Pursuit of fantasy goals (the ones gathering dust in the attic of your mind!)

Then, once again, write your day in the life. The most important tips are:

- *Write in the first person*
- *Weave in the changes you've listed – but capture fresh ones as they come up*
- *Make it achievable, but push out the boundaries*
- *Have fun*
- *Don't compromise on the really important issues*

Use the same principles as for the current story: revisit, add to, tidy up (but not too much), and allow the themes to incubate in your mind. Remember the warning against not letting the light into the camera too early. Take care who to discuss your story with, and at what point it's right to do so.

Now you're ready to start bringing your story to life. But even before you start acting, be aware that the tale has already started working in your mind. If your deepest intention is that you can turn the ideal into the real, you will soon start noticing the patterns you need to change and fresh opportunities will start to present themselves to you. The process of translating re-thinking into action begins the minute you set pen to paper.

Living your story

Let's return to the rich metaphor of thinking of your life as a story, in particular the core story or the intuitively familiar 'mono-myth' that crops up in all cultures throughout all time. In this simplified version the stages are:

- The quest
- Setting out
- Meeting obstacles: witches, trolls and giants
- Finding helpful agents: magic weapons, spells and allies
- Achieving the quest
- Returning home with the boon

The quest

Questions that spring to mind when we think of a quest are:

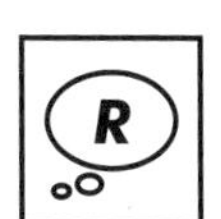

- *Do you have a clear quest or series of quests in your life?*
- *What is your 'Holy Grail'?*

In other words, what are the higher aspirations you have that you may have parked somewhere and forgotten, even for decades? You can use the story method in this chapter for capturing your quest, with greater ambition than Frank's story. His was more to do with lifestyle and quality of time than achieving his higher goals.

The steps for writing it are the same, but the questions that guide your story will be more profound. Questions like:

- How do I see the life I know I should be leading?
- What would it mean to live more creatively?
- What's my purpose in life?

Here you may need to solicit help to get out of your own 'box', perceptions that may be limiting you. 'I'm too old', 'It's too late', 'I could never …' are typical of the tapes that may be playing in your head. These will prevent you from even setting out.

However, beware the overnight celebrity trap. Watching TV talent programmes – *Pop Idol, The X Factor* and the like – I'm struck by the sheer desperation of people to succeed and how they believe their whole life will be blighted if they don't get through each harrowing round. 'It's my dream,' they cry, using the most devalued word in the language. A mood of desperation – even desperate positive thinking – won't get you anywhere. Intentions that are maturing deep in your mind and heart will.

The other methods you could use for clarifying your quest might be to visualize or draw it, discuss it with a mentor or someone supportive. It's like your CV: *it should make you cringe slightly*. To be more practical, it's useful to make a list of the skills or abilities you have *separate from the job you are now doing.* This will give you a fresh angle to weave into your story.

Setting out

There's a joy in starting anything. The trick is not to delay until the conditions are perfect. What's fundamental to making your first steps a success is the quality of attitude and energy you project into it.

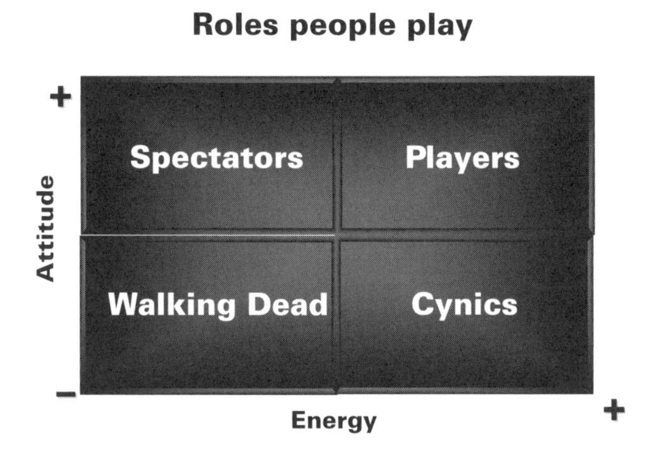

A simple way of capturing this is the visual above, which I've used with individuals and groups to get them to assess their level of commitment to a set of goals or quest.

Obviously you're not going to go very far on our journey if you're sleep-walking – like the walking dead – into the future. But more dangerous is to play the role of a spectator, seeming to say all the right and positive things, but not possessing the energy to take risks and try things out.

Being a cynic is an easy box to fall into. People in organizations counter new ways of working from this perspective, castigating anything new as 'flavour of the month'.

In contrast, to be a player means to be a hero or heroine in pursuing your goals. Fortune certainly favours the prepared mind, but it also favours those with the energy to act. When artist Damien Hirst was challenged by a critic who said, 'I could have done what you've done', Hirst responded, 'Yes, but you didn't – *I* did.'

Being a player means setting out on the journey with the same optimistic spirit as the Little Tailor in the fairy story. To stride out as a player means not just having a patina of positive thinking, which for many is just positive *hoping*, but with a conviction that when you fail at some stages of the journey you will not just revert to the other boxes. Real positivity means *belief* in your ability to create success.

I once asked a great spiritual teacher what he regarded as the secret of success in life. I expected some gnomic *koan* or aphorism, but he merely said:

> *'Persistence. Persistence. Persistence.'*

Meeting obstacles

This is where your desire to be a player will be tested the most. If you don't meet any obstacles, it's a sign that you're not tackling something ambitious enough!

Avoid naïvety and realize that there is a dark side – psychologically often called the shadow – of human nature. Attempt to change something, and you will almost certainly make enemies.

You may find it a bit strong to use the language of witches, trolls and giants, but in terms of achieving your quest, this is just what they are.

There are two ways of dealing with obstacles. You can have an expectation of success, or one of failure. Let's assume you experience a setback on your journey. The measure of how much of a hero you are is not that this occurs, but how you deal with it. If your underlying view is a failure mindset, you will find yourself thinking:

- I knew it wouldn't work.
- Luck is what happens to other people.
- It's not what you know; it's who you know.

This mindset views success as attributable to outer factors and will find it difficult even to enjoy the fruits of deserved success.

Contrast this with having an unreasonable expectation of success, but encountering failure nonetheless. This kind of person responds with thinking:

- Persistence, persistence, persistence!
- Let's try another way.
- Time yet not invested, skill not yet acquired.

Of course, the significant word in the last sentence is 'yet'.

The important thing is to be aware of which of these views is driving us. Naturally, a player is someone who adopts the positive expectation and feeds this belief deep within him/herself by celebrating each step of success and revisiting each failure with renewed heroic energy.

Finding helpful agents: magic weapons, spells and allies

Help is all around us, but we may not know how to ask. Many people are not good at asking for it, even in a world where life coaches are ten a penny. It's still perceived, particularly by men, as a sign of weakness or inadequacy.

If your quest is ambitious, spend time finding these helpful agents now!

The wise old man or woman of a fairy tale is what we can call in everyday life a mentor. In your professional life, you may have been assigned a mentor. But my experience is that this works far less well than when you seek one out for yourself. It's often someone you already know, but haven't thought of in this context before. A wise relative, a supportive friend who may know little about your job, but takes a great deal of interest in you as a person.

Above all, one kind of magic that will help you in your quest comes from deep and meaningful friendships. True friendship is rare – the people who confuse acquaintances with friends are often lacking in the ability to develop real intimacy with others. At times of great stress people find the least amount of time to contact their 'helpful agents', which is just the time they need them the most. In time-use terms, you have to make it important *and* urgent.

The magic of self-belief

Be careful when seeking help from mentors, experts, or even some friends, that you don't give away your own personal magic. Too often we abandon this when we are with people who seem to be more intelligent or knowledgeable than ourselves. Did you ever have the intuition that your lawyer, architect or accountant wasn't going about things the right way, but resigned yourself to their supposedly superior abilities? We give away too much of our personal power when we rely on experts. Our real power comes from reminding ourselves that our journey is uniquely ours and that at some level we *know* the right course of action. Mentors are valuable when they help us open doors in our own mind rather than just giving advice.

Achieving the quest

The idea of breaking down your quest into stages has been covered already. It's vital to regenerate your enthusiasm for the quest at these key milestones.

> *Celebrating what you* have *achieved rather than obsessing about what you haven't is necessary to keep you on the journey.*

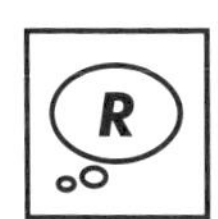

This advice is particularly true for perfectionists. Perfectionism in itself is a great trait, but not when it prevents you from having any of the joy that comes with completion. Very often someone else needs to wake you up from the quest you have been too close to in order to congratulate you, or allow you to congratulate yourself.

It's wonderful to see the joy on an athlete's face when they've just run the fastest 100 metres in the world, or the bliss and relief for a mountaineer who's just climbed Everest. Most of our quests will not have contained within them that obvious pinnacle of achievement, so we need to build it in ourselves.

> *Ways in which you can achieve this are to treat yourself to a perfect evening, to something you've always wanted to do or have. Best of all is to throw a party.*

If your quest has been huge, there will always be recognition that in the field of activity there is so much more to do. Enjoying the moment and sharing it with others you care for or who have come with you on the journey is not the same thing as resting on your laurels.

Bringing home the boon

This overlaps with the notion of celebrating success, but there is something more profound to do here. It's reflecting on how well you've done, and of course what you can learn to take on the next journey. The theory sounds easy, but too much of life today is moving on to the next big thing without taking some time, perhaps some solitude, to realize and enjoy what you have achieved and what allies, spells and magic you need for the next time. In a relaxed state, dwell on these words by poet Derek Walcott:

'Sit. Feast on your life.' [4]

Acres of gold

There's a story of a man who travelled the world unsuccessfully to find riches. After he died his son found that the family farm was built on acres of gold. Today, many of us make outer journeys to find treasure. As Carole King sings, 'Doesn't anybody stay in one place any more?' There's even an expression for trying to change your life by changing the location you live in – it's called 'doing a geographical'.

A simple idea comes from this story. It's that we will find most wealth by looking within or by thinking afresh about what's close at hand. Even finding treasure through non-action.

---

[4] From *Love After Love.*

re-think nine

Meditation

Thinking more deeply is a constant *Re-Think* theme. I don't mean it in a theoretical or academic way: I'm talking about the *experience* of quieter, more expanded and fluid states of mind that are arrived at most swiftly and reliably through meditation. And most effectively by the only type of meditation that's been subjected to 35 years of rigorous scientific research, the technique of Transcendental Meditation (TM).

Forget for a moment Eastern mysticism, chanting or strange body postures. TM is a simple and highly pleasurable mental technique that requires no belief system or lifestyle changes to bring its benefits. Practised for 15–20 minutes twice a day, sitting with eyes closed, it's an effortless and enjoyable process that can be slotted into any routine. You can meditate on the train, on a plane, in your bedroom, or in an office.

I practice TM twice a day to give me greater clarity of mind and energy, essential in my speaking and consulting work. After a particularly energetic session recently, my client said that it would be great if all his people could be 'on' whatever I was taking. I told him that it was just two daily periods of meditation.

Emerging from the inner silence of meditation is like having pulled back the arrow on the bow. The further back you pull it, the further forward it flies. The more deeply you rest in meditation, the more dynamic you are afterwards. I benefited from the experience so much that I trained to teach TM in the mid-1970s.

Meditating in his office is exactly what a famous practitioner of TM, Sir John Harvey-Jones, used to do in breaks in his busy schedule as chairman of ICI. He testifies publicly to the way in which TM stopped him 'going down the Victor Meldrew[1] route' and kept his mind alert. Having spoken on the same platform with him at a recent conference, I can agree with this assessment. His perceptions into the workings of a business are more profound than his persona as a TV business doctor enabled him to express.

An estimated 4 million people around the world from every walk of life, culture and religion – and from the ages of 5 to 100 – have learned TM, from builders to brain surgeons, sports stars, housewives and schoolchildren.

I learned TM as a student during my last months at Oxford University. I remember sitting quietly by a small gas fire to meditate for the first time, and although I retained awareness of where I was, it was as if my mind had settled down to the silent depths of an ocean. It felt like 'coming home', reminding me of states of great peace and contentment I had experienced as a child.

As I hadn't been to a lecture in the subject I was studying at university for some considerable time, I was both pleased and amazed at the ability I soon gained to take in and recall large amounts of information in a deeply relaxed way. I did quite well in the exams. I hadn't expected

---

[1] A very grumpy and narrow-minded elderly character in a British television programme, *One Foot in the Grave*.

anything from TM – indeed, I learned just because an enthusiastic friend had dragged me along to the first talk.

I'll briefly describe how TM works, what the research tells us about its effects on mind, body and behaviour, how it compares with other forms of meditation and, most relevantly, how it helps us to explore the more silent levels of the mind from where ideas (our 're-thinks') emerge.

How TM works

TM is taught in a systematic way. It is the practical aspect of the Vedic tradition (Veda simply means 'knowledge'), currently revived by the Indian philosopher and scientist Maharishi Mahesh Yogi. You learn to use a sound and think it internally in an effortless way. A commonly held misconception is that you have to clear the mind of thoughts: this will only give you a headache. Nor do you try to concentrate the mind or think of soothing images – this only keeps you on the surface of the mind.

What you *do* learn is a subtle but precise technique for thinking effortlessly. The effect of doing this is to allow the mind to become quiet and eventually transcend, or go beyond, the thought process itself, arriving at a state that physiologists have called 'restful alertness'. You're not in a trance; when I'm meditating on a train I'm able to give the inspector my ticket when he comes round, and I haven't missed my station yet.

When you come out of meditation your mind and body are charged with the qualities that are found in this experience of inner wakefulness: mentally clearer, less stressed, more energetic, and with your perceptions sharpened. Research has shown that your reaction time is faster after a period of TM (fall asleep in a chair and you're more sluggish for a while), and colours seem brighter, smells and tastes richer. Quite simply you are resting your brain and body in a way that, as William Blake describes, 'cleanses the doors of perception'.

What you've been doing is allowing the body's innate intelligence to repair and restore itself. When I say TM is natural, this is synonymous with effortlessness, a principle that Nature follows in the law of least action, the most universal law in science. It's a re-think or reversal of the busy, surface level idea that doing more means achieving more: in meditation the theme is *do less and accomplish more*.

There's a very specific method you're taught for achieving this, but essentially, once you've learned, the only thing you can do wrong is to try. Putting in effort stops your nervous system from settling into the natural, but paradoxical, state of being deeply rested while mentally alert or awake inside. What keeps me making time for it on a daily basis after 30 years is that it's so easy and pleasurable as well as effective.

Research on TM

So many people were reporting anecdotally that they felt more creative, stress-free and, not to be underestimated, just plain *happier* after their practice of TM that scientists began as long ago as the 1960s to look for measurable changes in mind, body and behaviour. Were the benefits that people reported mere wishful thinking or a kind of placebo effect triggered by positive expectations?

The response is contained in over 500 published research papers in the major science journals of the world, including *The Lancet, Nature* and the *Journal of Neurophysiology*. Changes in the body that accompany the mind relaxing deeply are quite extraordinary: blood pressure normalizes, muscle tension dissipates, and there are short bursts of greatly increased blood flow to the brain. Interestingly, none of these changes are aimed for: they are a natural by-product of a pleasurable process that it seems anyone can learn easily.

The most important point is that changes in the physiology are cumulative and sustained outside the daily periods of meditation. These include marked declines in all of the signs by which we measure stress: high blood pressure, stress hormonal levels, cholesterol levels, measures of anxiety and dependence on drugs (prescribed or not), alcohol or tobacco. Several studies show significantly less need for doctors and hospitals and faster recovery from illness and operations. After all, the doctor's advice is often to 'get some good rest' – as a meditator, your body's intelligence has naturally learned how to accomplish this.

So at a time when rising health costs threaten to cripple even the largest economies and companies – GM's estimated annual health bill is $5 billion – it's not surprising that governments have taken a shrewd interest in the long-term benefits of sponsoring TM. The American National Institutes of Health (NIH) has spent $20 million in recent years into research on TM's beneficial effect in reducing blood pressure and a number of other factors that predispose individuals to heart disease.

Reversal of the ageing process

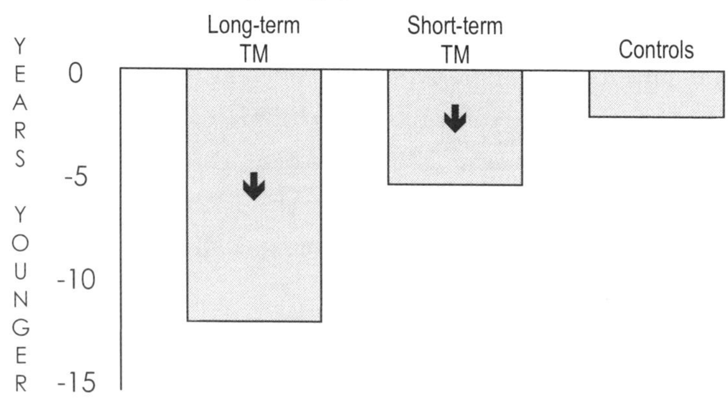

The Effects of the Transcendental Meditation and TM-Sidhi programme on the Ageing Process, *International Journal of Neuroscience* 16(1), 1982, pp. 53, 58.

A recent study confirms earlier research that TM may actually help you live longer![2] Dr Robert Schneider, who led the research, found that among older people with mild blood pressure those practising Transcendental Meditation had a 23 per cent lower risk of death from all causes. In this study some practised TM while a control group tried other techniques supposed to reduce stress, such as progressive muscle relaxation. The TM group had 30 per cent fewer deaths from heart disease and 49 per cent fewer from cancer.

What about the mind? Dramatic improvements in IQ, memory and learning ability have also been observed.[3] One that's particularly revealing for creativity is the improvement in 'field independence', the ability to pick out an embedded figure from a confusing background.[4] This parallels the subjective experience of meditators that they gain the ability to see problems from a clearer perspective. In psychological terms they are able to simultaneously maintain broad comprehension with sharp focus. In everyday language, this means that you can see the wood for the trees.

The most fascinating research comes from electroencephalographic (EEG) studies on the brains of meditators. This doesn't show anything as trivial as producing more alpha waves – we all do that when more relaxed, though only in the occipital cortex. Not only do the right and left hemispheres of the brain become more synchronized, but, more unusually, high levels of coherence are also found between the frontal 'executive' lobes and the rest of the cortex. In this state, a stimulus is processed by a much wider area of the brain and more quickly than usual. Together

---

2 Ref: the *Guardian*, 2 May 2005.

3 'Three Randomised Experiments on the Longitudinal Effects of the Transcendental Meditation Technique and Cognition', So K-T, Orme-Johnson, D., Intelligence, 29(5), September/October 2001 pp. 419–40.

4 'Field Independence, Transcendental Meditation and Achievement in College Art: A Re-examination', Fergusson, L.C., *Percept Mot Skills*, 77(3Pt 2), December 1993; pp. 1104–6.

with findings from neurotransmitter studies, this has led scientists to conclude that TM is a systematic way of allowing the brain to enter its own built-in fine-tuning mode, to grow and develop, overcome fixed patterns, form new connections, and function more fully.

Creativity and TM

Film director David Lynch, creator of *Twin Peaks, Blue Velvet, Mulholland Drive* and many other successful films, is a 30-year practitioner of TM. He explains what this means for his creativity:

'I see TM this way. If you have a golf-ball-sized consciousness, you will look at everything that way. TM expands your consciousness, so your experiences grow exponentially. As a film-maker, I tell stories, and with expanded consciousness, you catch bigger, deeper ideas. I have found that with TM intuition grows, too, and when you're working in film or even in business, intuition is a huge tool that makes it easier to deal with people.'

The Times, 'Body and Soul' supplement
3 September 2005, pp. 6–7.

Other forms of meditation

A systematic review of over 140 studies has shown that TM reduces anxiety twice as much as other techniques. Another found that it was three times more effective in cultivating self-actualization. This is a measure of overall personality development and maturity; it is characterized by greater fulfilment and peak experiences of transcendence in everyday life.

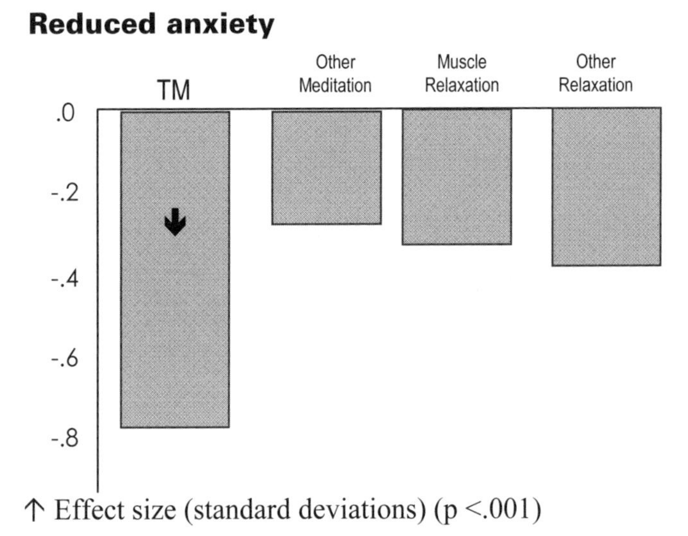

Differential effects of relaxation techniques on trait anxiety: A meta-analysis, *Journal of Clinical Psychology*, 45, 1989, pages 957, 974.

Ironically, one of the few things that gets me angry is unresearched and ineffective methods of stress management. TM is *not* the same as muscle relaxation, visualization, guided meditations, or the meditation you learn at the end of a yoga class. The differences may seem subtle, but the long-term effects are worlds apart. *In particular, if you have a book that claims to teach you to meditate ... put it in the bin!* It is inaccurate and preventing you from having a much deeper experience through a technique which has been taught for thousands of years through a precise oral tradition. Individual experiences of meditation vary, so it's essential to have a guide to explain it.

TM, creativity and re-thinking

Of course you don't become a creative genius overnight by learning a technique like TM. We all start from where we are. And some very creative people I have introduced to meditation notice a growing balance in other areas of their life. One famous musician said to me that the main benefit he noticed was being more emotionally at ease with others in a social setting. It seems that long-term meditation helps you to become more balanced, and different individuals gain what they need to achieve this. In a world where we value – indeed over-value – specialization, TM helps you to become a more rounded person, able to take what life throws at you with inner resilience. You become, to use that wonderful French expression, *bien dans sa peau.*

How does this equate with the common stereotype of the artist as a tortured individual, creating his or her best work due to heartbreak, poverty or crisis? This requires some re-thinking, as creativity is the product of an expanded mind, not a stressed one. For many, the art of creation is a *release* from the stress they experience, not a result of the pain but a channel for coping with it. Mozart's observation that ideas came to him best when he was relaxed, travelling at night in a carriage, is revealing.

People are not generally creative when they are depressed, a condition that has replaced neurosis as our most pervasive psychological dis-ease. Meditation helps over time to alleviate unnecessary depression, not to be confused with states of insightful melancholia.

The brain studies already described explain the subjective experience of meditators – that ideas just come to them more readily, less filtered and restricted by the anxiety that accompanies the desire to perform well in any field.

But creativity does require a *challenge*. I'm often faced with a potentially stress-creating situation in my work, for instance having to speak to 300 people in a company after lunch. I speak without a script, so I have to be very mentally tuned in. I find an extra 5-minute period of meditation prepares me for this both mentally and, just as important, emotionally. Emotional resilience and not being phased by what others throw at you is as important a benefit of the long-term practice of TM as the greater mental clarity that comes.

There's a vital distinction here between being nervous and being tuned in or fired up. You need the latter to perform at a high level in most activities – but being anxious doesn't help. This is simply described in the illustration below.

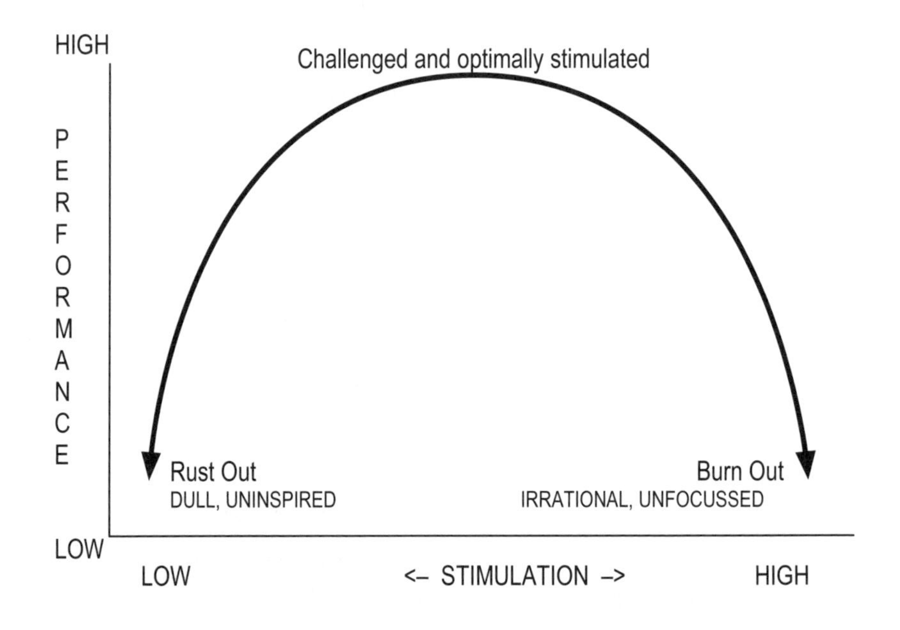

This is an intuitive way of understanding the balance you need to find in life as a whole and at specific periods of high performance. TM seems to help with this more than any other technique I'm aware of.

Are there any downsides? Well, if you just sat around all day and meditated it wouldn't necessarily bring you any greater benefits. A bit like taking all your medication at once: the body needs the natural rhythm of rest and activity, stillness and dynamism to integrate the effects of meditation. I notice the benefits of TM the most when I'm really busy. If I sound like a recruiter for TM, I don't excuse myself – I am.

The body 'remembers' the effects of meditation

Diving into deeper levels of thought and physical rest is what you experience during meditation. The everyday value is that some of this inner stillness stays with you even when you're running for a plane or bombarded with emails and phone calls. There's no belief involved here – you can *think* intellectually that the whole thing is nonsense, but provided you *experience* the systematic dissolution of stress that comes from regular meditation, your body and brain 'remembers' it for you as you just get on with life. So, no need to change your lifestyle, diet or belief system.

The fee for learning TM is not inexpensive, and the organization that teaches it has charitable status in many countries. Most people who continue to practise will say it's the most valuable thing they ever learned. The occasional accusation that TM is a cult is far-fetched. Most people learn the technique for practical benefits such as relieving stress and improving their creativity in everyday life. They practise it as a pleasurable daily routine that enriches their lives as students, housewives, managers, teachers or whatever. Cults condition you to think in certain ways, while meditation allows you to remove much of this conditioning and think for yourself, whatever field you're involved in. To take one example, a great hero of American football, Joe Namath, is a keen meditator who describes how TM helped him in his playing days to get into 'the Zone', that relaxed but focused state all players reach for.

I've talked about the *practical* benefits of meditation, and propose TM as a technique worth learning specifically because:

- It works!
- It's reliably supported by research, not just wishful thinking.
- It requires no belief, change in religion, lifestyle or diet.
- It's easy to learn.
- It's very pleasurable to practise.

Everyday spirituality

I wouldn't be doing the subject justice if I didn't mention the spiritual aspects of meditation. 'Spiritual' is a word that could be a contender for the most poorly understood and most argued-over concept in the history of mankind.

The most useful way to understand it is as 'wholeness', a word that is not accidentally related to the notion of holiness. Too much of religious thinking sees spirituality as somehow removed from, *other than*, our everyday life. It's hard to pin down and measure, and so in a rational age it's often labelled as mere belief, faith or hope, or even less usefully as something we can only experience after death. If anything is dangerous superstition, it's this notion that divides the mundane from the mysterious, the life we lead in the world from the life of the spirit.

Body rested, mind awake

Wordsworth, in his *Lines Written A Few Miles Above Tintern Abbey*, described a state where his breath and human blood seemed suspended. As a result:

While with an eye made quiet by the power
Of harmony, and the deep power of joy
We see into the life of things.

This is an experience that I and many people who meditate are familiar with, even though we may not have Wordsworth's gift of poetry to express it.

The spiritual poet Kahlil Gibran describes a way of bridging this division in his famous line that 'love is work made visible'. But we do not 'find ourselves' through work so much as by contacting our inner nature, the unchanging observer we come to know in moments of great stillness. Jesus tells us in the Gospel of Luke exactly where the heavenly experience resides when he says, 'The Kingdom of God is within you.'

A great misunderstanding perpetrated by many so-called spiritual teachers is that this inner state is a state of nothingness. What they are actually saying is that the meditative state is one of *no-thingness*. In other words, you have removed the senses during meditation from the outer world of things and phenomena, but the subjective experience is one of great fullness or happiness, not emptiness.

This is the essential teaching of all spiritual traditions, the direct inner experience of what we could call the level of Being. The message of TM is that you don't need to immerse yourself in strange philosophies to experience this. One company director that I was teaching creativity and meditation to put it this way after a few weeks: 'These days we are so busy Doing that we've forgotten what it's like just to Be.' A biochemist by training, he's not a man normally given to flights of fancy. To me he's expressing the notion of spirituality as wholeness: the flourishing of our inner and outer lives.

The biggest re-think that meditation gives us is that by turning our attention within, we can be more effective in tackling the problems that appear to be outside ourselves. Again, the French have a great expression for this: *reculer pour mieux sauter*. To withdraw in order to jump forward better. That's what meditation achieves.

RE-THINK NO. 18: JUST DO IT!

The worst thing you can do on the subject of meditation is to start reading books on the subject, especially if book worship gets between you and the experience of meditation. Experience is all.

Just contact a centre teaching TM and do it. And the less you do, the more you will be able to accomplish. That's how Nature works and therefore how our nature works.

re-think | ten

You, me, us – relationships

'All has to do with loving and not loving,' observed the mystic Rumi several centuries ago. More recently, it's been said that relationships are the yoga of the West. Our obsession with them certainly seems to bear this out.

Whenever I've been doing career counselling – sometimes more sexily called 'performance counselling' – by the third meeting the real concern emerges. It's usually to do with relationships. It seems that jobs may be tough but manageable, the children frustrating but worth it. What throws a shadow over it all is so often the question of the prime relationship, or new relationships that seem to be offering themselves.

We're told that all families are dysfunctional – whatever that means – and the divorce rate is more than 1 in 3 in the UK, higher among younger couples. It's nearly 50 per cent in the USA. The emotional and economic costs are at almost epidemic level, though not all of this is bad. In the past people would stay in unsatisfactory relationships for social ('No one in *my* family has been divorced!') or economic reasons, or 'for the sake of the children'.

Today we have a different problem, the subtle but powerful pressure of choice – choice of partners, freedom to travel and meet new people, choice of same sex partners, relative wealth for many (though not for all) to cope with starting a new family and managing the complexities of a 'blended family' with children from past relationships. Choice is a two-edged sword, particularly as most of us aren't mature enough to handle it well.

The paramount importance of relationships is what made me write this chapter. It kept cropping up in other sections I was writing and I thought it would be sheer cowardice not to apply re-thinking to it. But any sane person should be somewhat wary of writing about this subject, especially if they are therefore taken as an expert on relationships. How frequently have you seen or read about golden couples writing books and running workshops on how to improve your marriage, who are then divorced before you know it.

We should start with what I called earlier Open-Page thinking, the beginner's mind of the amateur. We think we know more than we do about what makes a great relationship and probably believe we are more of an ideal partner than is the reality. So rather than give a set of prescriptions for the ideal relationship – in our turbulent times I'm not certain this exists – this chapter is six brief journeys into different re-thinks you can use as appropriate.

First, some essential principles:

You are the expert

Only you are the expert on your own relationship. You may get advice, but only you are the one living it who knows its unique meaning, twists and turns, joys and annoyances. You alone are the player that can create the circumstances you need to thrive. If you've become like the walking dead, a spectator or cynic in your prime relationship, you will watch it slide away from you. Your relationship is unique – you make the rules.

No one can fully understand another's relationship from the outside. That's why the onus is on you. Both of you, of course.

There's no ideal

There are as many different relationships as there are couples (or threesomes!). Some work very well living in separate houses, or spending time apart (a friend tells me this is the secret of his mostly happy long-term marriage). Others are inseparable: Paul McCartney and his late wife Linda spent only seven nights apart in their long and much-travelled marriage. Don't try to fit your unique view of a good partnership into someone else's.

Relationships need refreshing

Relationships need maintenance, refreshing, reaffirming, honest acknowledgement of changes – her new career, the arrival of children, the demands of different stages of life and so on. We've lost many of these rituals, so we need to rediscover these or create new ones.

A deeper purpose

There are spiritual reasons for being a couple that we seem to have forgotten. For instance, the principle of giving of ourselves fully has been diminished, partly by the psychology of self-assertion ('Getting What You Need From Your Marriage' type self-help books) and by our high expectations of what we will gain from the set-up.

Real giving doesn't look for its reward. Conditional giving can quickly turn into a calculation about 'what's my return on the investment here?' or even long-term self-pity, moving in the direction of martyrdom. If you feel unappreciated, and as if your partner – or indeed life – owes you a lot, you're on the martyr's path. It's not very attractive – to you or your companion.

I've often been put off the idea of '*working* on a relationship' simply because of associations with the word 'work'. Shouldn't a marriage be a respite, a safe haven from the tribulations of 'work', whether in the office or the home? There may be work involved but I'd like to add the companion concept of playing in a relationship. Not of course in the sense of toying with it or 'playing around' (it's surprising how many negative associations come with the word play) but by rediscovering or remembering that a sense of joy, of playfulness together is what probably attracted you in the first place. Couples who play together are more likely to stay together.

If you work – or play – on one of the principles above, you will find the effect spilling over into the other areas. Think of pulling a chair by one leg and you naturally find the others follow.

These concepts are woven into the six re-thinks that follow.

Appreciating yourself

We all see the world as we are. We know this intellectually, but often forget that the world we see is the world we make. Therefore, we can only appreciate or love another to the extent that we appreciate ourselves.

To give a simple example, a client of mine in the public sector gave a talk – not a bad one, I thought – and asked his staff to rate it. He was upset to see that one man had given him 1 out of 10, and had added the comment: 'I thought this was much better than last year when I gave you a zero.' My observation was that this person's life experience was probably only 2 or 3 out of 10, and that he probably wouldn't know a 5 or 6 if he saw one. Did it make the speaker feel better? Not a lot! But it's clear that we will only be able to rate others as we see or value ourselves.

It's harder to give to others if we don't value ourselves. An attractive, intelligent, newly divorced friend told me that her first impulse was to think that if a man was interested in her, there must be something wrong with him! As long as she has this mindset about herself, relationships will be less likely to develop.

Let's start with the outer self, how we look and how we dress. If we appreciate ourselves we'll look good for our partner. It's so easy to let ourselves slide and wear things in front of our loved one that we'd never be seen dead in at work. (Writing this section caused a considerable re-think of my own wardrobe, so I'm writing this as an offender rather than an expert!)

I used to sneer at TV programmes that encouraged people, particularly women, to dress better. On UK television you'll find Trinny and Susannah, a sometimes quite brutal couple who make over people's dress sense and general appearance. But after reading some of their book, I realized that it's not about style or being fashionable but about *self-esteem*. Their cleverness is to advocate a look that is adapted for the individual, many of whom are not conventionally glamorous, beautiful or wealthy. Often the women cry at the gap between how they have become and how they can be with a little assistance, and many of the new items of clothing are inexpensive. Men need an equivalent programme!

This may seem a superficial approach to self-appreciation, but it's a practical starting point. I've emphasized throughout *Re-Think* how the inner is the basis of the outer: the outer certainly affects the inner as well. It's about care, attention and the sickly sounding but very necessary requirement to do some self-loving. Only a few have the opposite problem of narcissism, so I'd advocate a daily dose of self-appreciation in front of a flattering mirror. You'll soon be told if you've gone too far.

Self-appreciation means having the courage to wear your clothes and hair in a way that suits you individually. Style, not fashion.

And to regard every day as an occasion, not saving up your best for that special event that so rarely comes around.

Beauty in daily life shouldn't be so hard to find, and I think Trinny and Susannah's bold stand against the omnipresent black – to most people *black* is the new black – is a great re-think.

Moving beyond outer appearances, appreciation of your *qualities* is where your friends come in. Or should. Really hearing their appreciation of your good attributes can help enormously, provided you can switch off the voice in your head that says 'yes, but ...' One of the most embarrassing questions you can ask a friend is to tell you what they appreciate about you, both as a friend and a person. Which is what makes it such a relief and a breakthrough to hear. If they can't do it, they may not be the friend you thought they were. The secret is to listen in silence and accept the gift from them. Let the other's perceptions sit with you for a while and soak into your roots before your critical inner censor can undermine this positive message. Thank them, but don't feel you have to respond to them in a similar vein at this time – save it for another occasion so you don't dilute what you are receiving.

The joys of feedback?

'Feedback' is a word due for re-thinking. It should be neutral – consultants of the psychological variety claim that 'feedback is a gift'. But if I were to say to you, 'I'm going to give you some feedback', would you feel your heart warming because you were about to receive a gift? No! You'd sense that something critical or diminishing was about to come your way.

Feedback in this sense is rarely a gift: in part because the person giving it may not have the requisite skills to make the perception useful to you, and also because it may be about something beyond your power to change. For instance, 'you're too tall', 'too angular', 'too intense'. I'm not saying be dishonest, but to err on the side of appreciation rather than criticism is a fruitful mistake to make. Swallow the 'but' that comes to your mind more often.

Now you are more in the mood to appreciate others.

Appreciating another

When we fall in love we are almost all prey to selective and self-centred perception. At last I've met someone with style, humour, intelligence, good values, good looks – someone *just like me*. The points of difference, other habits, opinions or beliefs are screened out in the glow of what we take to be true love. These same differences may give therapists enough material to work on for the next 20 years!

Because after, say, six weeks, we start noticing these signs of otherness. We are no longer 'falling in love,' but we have begun the much more difficult – and ultimately more rewarding – journey of loving another *as they are*. Therapists are used to hearing her say 'If only he would talk!' or him saying 'I don't know what she wants', ad infinitum. Let's start with the harsh but realistic view that he or she probably isn't going to do any of these things. And begin by reaching out ourselves.

From a spiritual point of view there's a higher purpose to a relationship than comfort, security, the parenting of children and so on. It's a chance to practise in an intimate setting the path to a higher consciousness of unity. I'm not asking you to adopt any specific belief system here, rather I'd like to touch into your innate feeling that there is something bigger than our own needs and more expanded than our normal sense of self. We could call this in its highest form 'service', in the way that Albert Schweitzer meant when he said:

> *'I don't know what your destiny may be, but one thing I know. The only ones among you who will be really happy are those who have sought and found how to serve.'*

It's significant that he equates happiness with service. Built into the notion of giving to another is that you receive from service, from your own giving.

A good starting point is appreciation.

Observe your own inner dialogue about your partner and reflect upon what percentage of it is positive and how much critical.

More difficult is to discern how much of this can be put down to how you feel about life, coloured by your own frustrations and annoyances and projected on to the person you are most intimate with. Honesty is certainly the best policy in this case, though it's hard to stand outside yourself and gauge it. But it starts with you.

The next step is more concrete.

Find the time, the right space, to tell your loved one what you most appreciate about him or her.

This doesn't need to be a solemn occasion, but should be one in which you have the other's full attention. Often there will be laughs – if only to overcome the initial embarrassment of doing something you may not have done for years. Sometimes, even, since you got married. But don't let the humour degenerate into mere banter because this trivializes the tender message you are putting over. The conversation shouldn't then continue into any critical areas as to how you'd like to see more of that quality in your intimate life – that's for a follow-up discussion. Appreciation should be untouched by any qualification.

If this seems naïve, it is. It's using the principle of the second element from Chapter 4, 'Paying attention'. This is the idea that problems are not solved on their own level, but by moving towards the light rather than working in the darkness, a new set of solutions becomes available to you. Naïvety works much better than calculation and measuring in relationships.

Speak well of others

When we criticize others, we take on more of the energy of disappointment, doubt and distrust. *Try speaking well of others for a single day.* Unless you are a saint, it's far harder than you think. And also far more rewarding.

This kind of conversation may be out of character for you, or you may be rusty at it, so be prepared for your partner to say, 'What do you want from me?' It's unlikely – you'll be surprised at how cynicism melts in the face of real, heartfelt appreciation. But if this comes up there's really only one answer: 'Your love'.

Giving needs its counterpart, receiving, to have its full effect. If you've hardened yourself to receiving positive comments, often due to past disappointments in life or love, then not surprisingly this becomes a self-fulfilling prophecy: you filter out another's warm feelings and as a result people stop directing them your way so often. If you defend yourself against love and praise then your own self-worth is diminished. Learn to receive as well as to give.

Have that difficult conversation

Fairly soon a third person may enter your relationship. By this I don't mean a lover, but a kind of shadow that is fed by all the unspoken thoughts, unacknowledged and possibly negative feelings. This 'person' separates you, is with you at dinner and in the bedroom and may eventually obscure your view of those great qualities that drew you to the other at the outset.

It's especially evident in those partnerships that break up to the complete shock of one of the parties, often the man. 'I didn't think we had any serious problems' is frequently the plaintive cry. 'She never said …' But were you really there to hear it?

The conversation *is* the relationship

Poet and brilliant speaker David Whyte expresses this need for meaningful conversation concisely: She wants to have the conversation and he groans inwardly: didn't we do that last week, or when we first got together? What he's failed to realize is that for her the relationship *is* the conversation, and by the time he's ready for it, perhaps in his mid-forties and going through his own changes, it's often too late. Or she may have found another to have the conversation with.

Although this is quite unlike the appreciation session proposed earlier, it should still be undertaken in a spirit of respect. The feeling tone is what the other responds to more than the words, which is why you might usefully adopt the position of talking about the third person, the relationship itself, rather than the shortcomings of your partner.

But if you have to get into specifics that upset or deeply annoy you, try to separate the behaviour from the person. For instance, prefer 'I'm hurt that you never look at me when you come home from work', to 'you're so self-absorbed these days'. A person can change their behaviour – they can't so easily change their state of mind.

Also in this example you have made the mistake of imputing motives to another. These need to be spoken by the individual who owns them as only they know (if indeed they are aware) of what is on their mind that's preventing them from fully attending to the relationship. Be careful not to use absolutes like 'you *always*' or 'you *never*'. These can be called 'pig' words because they gobble up everything in their vicinity. Also, they are factually untrue and divert the flow of positive emotion. The simple advice is to be hard on the problem, soft on the person. Not an easy or comfortable thing to do, especially as so many currents of feeling will be flowing beneath the surface of your words.

The most important point is to finish the discussion, if not in resolution, but on a constructive note. People remember, emotionally as well as mentally, the first and last themes of an interchange, a film, book or presentation. The positive note could take the form of acknowledging that you truly care for and love the other and that's your motivation for having the conversation in the first place.

> *There are many books on how to have this kind of conversation – my suggestion is that you find one good one, read it and practice it together, make someone else's theory (far removed from the heat you are feeling!) your own practice.*

There's no right way, but you have to find a way together that doesn't wait until you are both beyond reconciliation. Occasionally have one of these conversations when things are going well.

It's vital to realize that when you are not open to this kind of conversation, the unseen but very real shadow begins to take over; you let unnecessary negativity in and, most seriously, in rejecting the other's need to talk, you are rejecting them.

Refreshing love

While it's easy to remember that the car or house needs maintenance, it's a little more complex to realize that our relationship also requires ongoing attention. One of the great things about family life is its beautiful messiness, the competing demands of partner and children, the trials and joys of the unexpected.

But what we lose sight of in this mess is how to be *fully present* for our loved one. I've rarely heard one half of a couple complaining that their partner gives them too much undivided loving attention!

'You don't listen' is one of the most commonly heard criticisms. Wily men will use the excuse that they were listening to the news or thinking about work and because they can't multi-task like women they couldn't pick up her plea for attention from all the background noise. A male friend told me that even making bacon *and* eggs at the same time was multi-tasking, and as a man the task was beyond him!

Naturally, the biggest gift is really being present for the other. This is why couples, particularly those with demanding jobs or offspring, need to carve out time and create their own rituals where they can fully attend to the other. Remember the original sense of 'attend' – 'to stretch to' – and practice it.

There are a number of ways to achieve this:

Find time together alone, rather than time alone together!

One of the most worrying sights is a couple who have been together for many years sitting in a restaurant with nothing to say to each other. Now while I'm prepared to accept the power of non-verbal communication, and sometimes sensitive enough to note the difference between a dull silence and a close couple just enjoying being in the moment together, all too often it's just that they are out of the habit of being together and enjoying each other's company. Practice now before it's too late.

I recently met a husband and wife who had hugely benefited from being part of a television programme where they swapped roles. A useful idea they learned was to spend what they rather cornily called Wonderful Wednesdays together – one evening a week where they packed the kids off to bed early, watched something special together or went out for a meal.

Now this sounds so obvious that part of me is embarrassed to write it – *except* that I see so many relationships where people have forgotten to be together – alone! A distance of only weeks or months in which you've had so many experiences and thoughts means it's too late to share them. The moment's gone. Which is why I start with the idea of a *routine* of being together, one evening or afternoon a week, in the hour before bed (and before you're too tired!) or whenever. Whatever you choose, create your own rituals and time together when you can give and receive the other's attention.

Revisit your vows.

It may be a long time since you made your initial vows, either in a formal marriage ceremony or perhaps just the commitments you made when you started living together.

If you don't have any, now might be the time to start. Accepting the principle that every relationship is unique, I believe that as well as the standard religious or social commitments, you should invent your own. My own example, as discussed in Re-think 11, 'Family rituals' (p. 120), is to say yes to using our marriage being a commitment to include and help others.

Examples of areas you might consider are:

- Attitudes towards children
- Emotional support you will give to each other
- Anniversaries you intend to mark in a special way

- Your beliefs about what the relationship is *for*
- Ways in which you intend to enrich each other's life

You might want to find occasions to speak these out and remember them from time to time, perhaps over dinner or on a long walk together. Or, if you're feeling bolder, you could adapt the idea from a couple I know who have been married for 25 years, with the usual ups and downs. They held a beautiful ceremony in which their grown-up children took part, reaffirming their original vows and introducing some new ones. What you agreed at the naissance of a marriage may need re-thinking, particularly when you've moved through so many stages of life together.

Invent loving surprises.

Harold Pinter's play *The Lover* contains a wonderful example of refreshing love. The man leaves home for work in the morning, sneaks back disguised as his wife's lover in the afternoon to enjoy passionate embraces, returns to the office and comes home in the evening as her loving husband.

Don't take this too literally! What it should make us think is that the different roles we play can become very stereotyped. There are probably more cynical jokes about how marriage can kill love than almost any other area of life. By being prepared to slip into different roles you can bring a freshness to your love.

One of the best surprises my girlfriend (as she then was) gave to me for a birthday was to turn up with a football team of friends – I was playing a match at the time – all dressed up in 1920s team uniform. Male and female members of the team were adorned with full kit, false wigs and beards. The pitch invasion turned into a wonderful free for all, and even though I temporarily lost credibility as a midfield hard man with the lads, it was a memorable surprise. As was the meal by the river afterwards.

One note of caution. I know people who do *not* enjoy surprises (I do!) so you have to be careful that what you scheme will be appreciated. But above all, if we can apply the same creativity to celebrating special occasions in our relationships that we probably do in our professional life, we don't have to think of being with another as merely 'settling down'. It's an interesting expression, isn't it? Try 'settling *up*' instead: keep finding fresh experiences to enjoy together and you're less likely to become set in a predictable routine with nothing new to know or to look forward to from your partner.

Say 'Yes'

This is the simplest and most direct of these re-thinks.

Your first response or reflex should be 'yes'.

Why?

Emotions are so volatile in any strong relationship that saying no contains an element of rejection, even if it's just a suggestion like 'should we go for a walk?' A 'no' can be taken as a small rejection of self. Intellectually we can unravel the part that means no to our idea, not to ourselves, but when did the intellect alone create a fulfilling marriage?

A few hours later, especially if it's a bigger idea like 'let's move to France', you may choose to express your reservations. Some of us are instant responders, some of us like to mull over an idea. By this time you may be surprised to find the other more open to a calmer discussion of the subject. It's so easy to kill another's enthusiasm by your initial expression of 'no' or, just as sapping, plain indifference.

What you are really saying yes to is the other's investment in the idea as much as the notion itself. Stop being a blocker and you will find that your partner can enrich your life and even lead you into new adventures.

Saying yes goes deeper than language or body language (though don't underestimate that in your responsiveness to fresh ideas). It's really about saying yes to your companion's imagination, to their integrity and sense of self-esteem. If you are more spiritually minded, you might say it's about affirming their essence, something we may choose to call their soul. Saying yes is harder to do than it sounds, but also surprisingly effective for demonstrating love and support.

Embrace the difference

Another way of appreciating difference is to value the masculinity or femininity of your partner. This can be more troublesome than it sounds because of the current trend to minimize the differences. This stems from social changes, particularly the emergence of successful women into many areas of life considered a solely male province. Also to political correctness, where a man feels he should display the same sensitivity as his female counterpart, whereas a woman is expected to be Superwoman.

We are muddled by stereotypes. Wanting to break free from the old patriarchal mindset of the authoritarian father and the submissive, frayed wife, we have replaced them with cardboard cutouts that don't do justice to the authentic differences of the sexes.

According to Eastern philosophy the man has a grosser nervous system while the woman's is more delicate. These are shocking words to say to a unisex generation, but there is no judgement, rather a clear assertion of what is. Feminism has quite rightly revised our awareness of the injustices inflicted on women, but biology is usually stronger than ideas, even in a Western world pervaded by unisex hegemony.

More delicate actually means more refined, perhaps less strong in a physical sense but more flexible and open to feelings, insight and intuition. Man's strength is focused but shorter lived – women still outlive their male partners by several years. Most women want their men to be stronger, not in a physical sense, but in a mental and emotional manner. Similarly, mature men are not threatened by a 'strong woman', but admire the feminine ways of expressing strength. Because women do need to be better than men to thrive in the professional world, some choose to adopt the demeanour and language of men. This is a tragic state of affairs, but it's not useful for either sex to blame the other.

When a book on an interesting topic is panned by the critics the contrarian in me makes me buy it. For men I can recommend nothing better on the subject of manhood than American poet Robert Bly's *Iron John*.[1] The central message is that in the Western world we have no rites of passage into manhood. Far from blaming women for this, Bly describes how the 'Loss of father' in our society means that growing men have few male role models to lead them into becoming men. He's acerbic about leaders who are happy to send young men to their deaths in war, while ensuring their own offspring are protected.

He explores cultures where the elders would take young men into the wilderness, scare the life out of them and make their passage into manhood a significant and meaningful event. In contrast, he describes how our teenagers – especially boys – grunt and hang around their household kitchen rather than find their way in the world. Much of this he puts down to the alienation caused by our working parents. In too many cases the son cannot even describe what his father *does* – he's not asked to pass on a skill such as mending nets, farming or wall-building, and sees him only when he's tired from another day at the office, doing something intangible and unimaginable. 'Too little father' is a sad reality of our times.

---

[1] Robert Bly, *Iron John*: A Book About Men, Rider & Co., 2001.

Women are not instinctively attracted to men who have no idea what it's like to be a man. Not in a macho sense, but having the qualities of the masculine impulse – decisiveness, strength, courage and so on. The sensitive New Age guy who wants to do a lot of 'sharing' and talk things through continually is not what she wants.

One image in *Iron John* is particularly gripping – that of the male's need, as a rite of passage, to steal the key from under his mother's pillow. It's a metaphor taken from the Grimm Brothers' story *Iron Hans*, on which Bly's book is based. This stealing of the key will mean different things to different men, but for me it's the cutting of childhood ties with the mother and setting out on one's journey alone. With some men today it doesn't happen until their 50s, if at all.

I have less to say of the women's perspective simply because I'm a man and I believe women say it better. Clarissa Pinkola Estes, the author of *Women Who Run With the Wolves*,[2] has written a series of compassionate stories that mark a woman's rite of passage. I'm told by female friends that this is very supportive and enlightening, and because phases in life are more obviously marked in changes in a woman's body it may be that they are more in touch with this than men.

Certainly older cultures are sensitive in some ways to these rhythms and cycles, advocating for example that a couple shouldn't make love for a number of days surrounding the woman's period. This is an acknowledgement of her essential difference that should be honoured, though in the First World there's a tendency to override these natural cycles. Perhaps a manifestation of the driving belief of consumerism that everything should be available anytime.

---

[2] Clarissa Pinkola Estes, *Women Who Run with the Wolves: Contacting the Power of the Wild Woman*, Rider & Co., 1998.

Embracing difference is a form of both/and thinking. Only when women are more secure in being women and men have remembered how to be men can a relationship be a real joining of opposites. In the same way that a flower can only manifest its whole beauty through the contrasts of leaf, thorn, colour and petals, love can only truly flourish when it's a reaching out to otherness, a unity of difference. We need to find a way of being in tune with these natural principles, though in an enlightened manner that honours rather than subjugates the differences.

RE-THINK NO. 19: RELATE!

Appreciating yourself

> *Go and spend whatever is a large amount of money for you – £50, £500, or more – on clothes you both feel and look good in.*

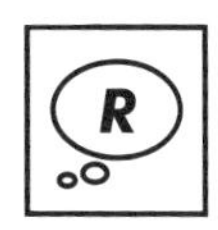

Remember, it's style not fashion, style that suits *you*, not some stereotypical ideal, and not something you're just doing for best. Take along a friend whose dress sense you admire.

Work out who you would like to gain positive feedback from (about your personal qualities, not just your clothes!). Put your embarrassment in the drawer for an hour and afterwards write down for your eyes only a list of your positive attributes. Do not allow yourself to censor or qualify this by writing, 'I'm *quite* good at …' or 'I'm *rather* successful at …' Take it out occasionally and read it over your morning coffee.

Appreciating another

This may require rehearsal – not too much or you'll lose spontaneity, but enough so you can *start* the discussion confidently. If you're too daunted by this you might be the sort of person who prefers putting things in writing. Remember – appreciation should be untouched by any qualification or deviation on to other topics. It's important enough to stand alone.

Have that difficult conversation

To be successful you have to find both the time and place. Too many of these important discussions start when one party is tired or the other is pressed for time.

Find a time and environment when it can be concluded without interruption from children or others and make sure you start and end with a declaration of your positive hopes for the relationship: people remember, emotionally as well as cerebrally, first and last impressions.

Refreshing love

Here your imagination's the limit! It might mean revisiting places where you had great times together in the past. Or something more elaborate like a surprise *This Is Your Life* event where you bring together many people from your partner's past and present.

Most of all, you want to create something that uniquely suits your partner. But even more important than the event is the way you demonstrate attention to the other's needs.

Too often, the woman is left in charge of social engagements. The biggest gift of all might just be to do the whole thing with the same professionalism that you would apply to your job.

Refreshing love can start with the trivial and the mundane. Have you noticed that if a man clears up, he has to bring it to your attention? How refreshing if he just does it!

Say 'Yes'

Practice on small things first. Otherwise your partner will think, 'He/she's just read a book on this or been to a workshop!' Domestic arrangements and shared chores are good places to start.

> *If you're having trouble with this, try forming the word several times in front of a mirror while checking that your body is also saying 'yes'.*

Embrace the difference

This is best done in three ways. First, by realizing that you *are* different, and not spending time regretting that the other cannot be more like you.

Second, by allowing for the mystery between the sexes to be respected. There's a great emphasis today on the talking cure, in other words the verbalising of feelings. This is all well and good as we do need to become more articulate about our feelings. But we also need to acknowledge that we're always keeping part of ourself to ourself.

J M Barrie describes this beautifully in *Peter Pan* when he says that there was always a smile in the corner of Mrs Darling's mouth that Mr Darling could not reach. There's much psychological insight in *Peter Pan,* the loss of which I mourn in its Disneyfied form, however entertaining.

Finally, assuming there is some depth to your relationship, the *personality* of your partner was no doubt a strong attractor in the first place. Re-think personality in its true sense: *per* means through, *sonare* means to sound. So it's not surprising that we use the language of sound when describing relationships – being in harmony, in tune, finding the right rhythm of life together.

What sounds through you when you speak to your loved one? Is it a sweet sound, or staccato and harsh? The differences can combine to produce a small symphony, and a lot of this comes from spending enough downtime together. I would rather call this 'in time', when you are really in and present for the other.

Whether you and your partner sound in harmony is an intuitive way of understanding your complementary or conflicting nature.

By changing your own tone, sound or rhythms, you can become closer to a loved one.

re-think eleven

The biggest re-think of all

The best re-thinks come from not taking a situation at its face value. Going deeper and discovering what is hidden always yields fresh ideas.

Albert Einstein observed that a problem is rarely solved by working at the level it's formulated. Our best ideas come to us unbidden and mysterious, from the gap between two neurons in our brain and between one task and another. Between sleeping and waking, or in the silence that separates two thoughts.

We have to admit that there is something magical and mysterious about this process. Here's Einstein again, commenting in a way that may seem surprising if we have a strong stereotype of a scientist:

> *'The most beautiful emotion we can experience is the mystical. It is the sower of all true art and science. He to whom this emotion is a stranger is as good as dead.'*

Mere intellectual methods of improving creativity that operate on the surface of the mind are akin to shuffling round the chairs on the deck of the Titanic. To look deeper let's briefly explore the field that has probed furthest beyond the surface of reality: physics and, in particular, quantum physics.

We're at least 100 years out of date in the way we use our brains because we haven't yet digested the findings of quantum physics. Why should we? Simply because it tells us about more powerful and profound levels of the physical world which bear an uncanny resemblance to the deepest levels of our mind. Physics reveals that the apparently solid world we see, touch and feel is nearly all empty space, and that the whole universe can be understood as nothing but fluctuations or waves in underlying quantum fields.

A strange thing is happening, as scientific descriptions of the deeper levels of existence take on the language of the mystic or poet. Hear how renowned physicist Brian Greene describes recent findings in string theory physics:

> *'String theory tells us that the "stuff" of all matter and all forces is the same. Each elementary particle is composed of a single string – that is, each particle is a single string – and all strings are absolutely identical. Differences between the particles arise because their respective strings undergo different vibrational patterns. What appear to be different elementary particles are actually different "notes" on a fundamental string. The universe – being composed of an enormous number of these vibrating strings – is akin to a cosmic symphony.'*[1]

What's fascinating is that these modern descriptions of nature are paralleled by ancient texts, which are based on subjective rather than objective ways of exploring reality. For example, in the several thousand year old Vedic literature of India we read:

---

[1] *The Elegant Universe,* Brian Green, Random House, 2000.

> *'Mama chaiva shariram vai sutram ity abhidiyate'*
>
> *My body is called a string*

or

> *My body has the nature of a string*

Ancient sage Vashishta was also ahead of Einstein when he observed that 'mass is but sleeping energy'.

A coincidence? Highly unlikely. Influential physicists like David Bohm and string theory expert John Hagelin describe the remarkable point-by-point similarities between our thinking process and the quantum description of the universe, and suggest that exploring these links may be essential to our self-understanding.

We do partially remember a quantum view of the world when talking about our thought processes. We speak of being 'in tune' with another, 'on the same wavelength', or sensing 'the vibe' as soon as we walk into a room. We even have 'brainwaves'.

Unfortunately, we have separated the inner from the outer by giving greater credence to the observable and measurable methods of knowing – commonly called science – at the expense of more intuitive and subjective ways of gaining knowledge. This is not to belittle the tremendous discoveries of modern science. While it's fashionable to criticize it as reductionist and mechanistic – explaining the building blocks while losing sight of the building – we should remember that it has done a fantastic job in getting us this far. To be within sight of a Unified Field Theory that can potentially explain everything.

However, it's only one way of knowing. Again, language is the portal to re-thinking. 'Science' comes from the Latin meaning 'to know'; 'technology' is from the Greek *techne*, meaning art. Neither the Greeks nor the Renaissance thinkers saw the rift between art and science, outer and inner, subjective and objective means of gaining knowledge. Looking inside ourselves for answers is as valid a path as laboratory experiments.

We have become split off from or have forgotten these inner ways, living in thrall to the superstition of materialism. This means that if we can see and touch something, we believe it's somehow more real than our inner world of imagination, dreams, hopes and fears. But which is more real to you – the love you have for your children or a coffee mug?

'Split' thinking means operating only on the surface of the ocean of the mind. Look at our societies and you can see where that's got us, despite our brilliance in producing external technology. The world is fragmented into competing ideologies and faiths, haves and have-nots, us and them, man and nature.

The biggest split in thinking that afflicts us today is not Descartes' error – dividing our reason from our emotions – but the gap between knowing theoretically about our unlimited potential and experiencing it. *We are out of our own nature.* The split between man and the environment will not be resolved until this gap is closed, and until we develop an inner ecology of consciousness. Without this we will continue to be like inept and superficial gardeners, polishing the leaves of the plant instead of watering its root.

What does it mean to be 'out of our own nature'? When science looks out at the physical world it attempts to remove the observer – you and me – from the equation. One of the greatest revelations of the twentieth century was that this simply doesn't work. It's been known for about 80 years in physics that the very act of watching and observing an experiment affects the process being observed. It's called the

Uncertainty Principle, and if we can fully understand its implications, it will change fundamentally our view of how much we are the active creators of our own world.

If this sounds strange, then so do most great re-thinks or innovations at first glance. Even physicist Niels Bohr said:

> *'If quantum mechanics hasn't profoundly shocked you, you haven't understood it.'*

What has this got to do with re-thinking? Almost everything. When I say we are behind the times in the way we think, I mean we may theoretically 'know' that Newton's clockwork world with its predictable laws of motion is not really how it is at a deeper level, but that's what we see when we open our eyes. Nature as a series of fixed, separate, or sometimes colliding objects. But creative and more enlightened minds view the world from a level that is more connected, and are able to see underlying patterns and the unity of inner and outer.

Poets are able to encapsulate this wonderful experience of unity. Wallace Stevens writes:

> *I was myself the compass of that sea:*
> *I was the world in which I walked*
> *And what I saw or heard or felt came not but from myself;*
> *And there I found myself more truly and more strange.*[2]

When physics probes into the underlying levels of creation, it finds that two particles can be in the same place at the same time and substances can become super-fluid and flow out of containers they are put into. Particles are even able to tunnel through apparently solid matter. In other words, different laws of nature come into play.

---

[2] 'Tea At The Palaz Of Hoon', *Wallace Stevens' Collected Poems*, Faber & Faber, page 65.

It's the same with our minds: at finer levels of thought we can make connections between apparently unrelated ideas, be anywhere, and see the whole picture rather than the individual parts of a problem. Just as in the physical world, different laws are operating. Ideas from this more unified level of thinking really feel as if they come from quite a different place than our more mundane thoughts. They come from a part of the mind that is less bound and more free.

So the challenge in the twenty-first century is to find ways of becoming 'quantum physicists' in our own minds. To research the inner Unified Field where all ideas come from. In this way, Unified Field theory becomes Unified Field *practice*.

How can we do this? First, by realizing that our thinking has at its most refined level a quantum-like, unified character.

Second, by understanding that the observer does affect the observed, not just in test tube science, but also in the way that you or I see reality. The world is as we are. How we think about life and its challenges actually creates the possibilities we see or miss.

Finally, knowing that deeper levels of thought are more powerful than the surface levels. As in physics, many times more power is released by splitting an atom than by throwing an apple that is composed of those atoms. So at least we know *where* to look for these great and more powerful ideas. They are inside us.

The most fundamental re-thinks of the twenty-first century will not be in the field of outer technology, whatever amazing inventions we create. They will come from studying and experiencing the infinite possibilities latent in our own consciousness. In particular:

- Our ability to think and act from the level of wholeness, rather than in a split, fragmented fashion.
- Our relationship to our own nature, which is also the nature of all things.
- Our 'self-remembrance' of the eternal, underlying levels of existence.

It's sometimes said that 'the only constant is change'. This is logically nonsense – the only thing that doesn't change is the changeless, the silent witness inside ourselves that we intuitively know despite all the outer changes in our appearance and circumstances. This is the 'I' that Tennyson refers to when he says:

> *'Men may come and men may go, but I go on forever.'*

The biggest re-think of all is that I, the eternal part of me, is not a powerless, tiny cork bobbing on an ocean. You and I are greater than the oceans our minds encompass. In Sanskrit, a more reliably precise language than English, it's expressed as:

> *Aham Vishvam.*
>
> *I am the universe.*

Acting as if

If you believe you are creative, then you are more likely to be so. Simply because you will put yourself into more situations where your inner prophesy can be tested out. But if you *don't* believe this, there's still one hand left to play. It's 'acting as if'.

This is a technique used in coaching sports stars and performers in many fields. When you remember to 'act as if' you are in the state of mind or zone that's required to swing that club or racket in a perfectly focused or relaxed way. We can apply this to daily life: if we remember to act 'as if' today will be the most creative and successful day we have ever had, we are significantly maximizing our chances of this coming true.

There are two reasons why this works.

First, life is a series of discontinuities or fresh starts followed by inevitable plateaus. This is true in the growth of the human body where there are enormous brain spurts followed by periods of integration. Growth, either of an individual or a business, is not a smooth trajectory. So there is nothing unnatural – and it's never too late – to choose a fresh start and act as if today is going to be more fulfilling and creative than yesterday. We can make a leap today, whatever the past was like. Just having this intention will improve our luck.

Second, in acting as if, we remember that we are all pretenders. Have you ever thought that in your life or job you are less able than you pretend and are just waiting to be found out? But this pretending, acting as if, can be a rehearsal for success if we are prepared to swallow our fear and take the first step. This wisdom is captured in the following words from an unexpected source:

> *'What is wrong with being pretentious? I think you only achieve anything by pretending to achieve it in the first place. I pretended to be a musician and by that process became a musician. I pretended to be a grown-up and by that process grew up. I pretended to be a dad and then I became a dad.'*
>
> *Sting*

Appendix 1
The *Re-Think* research

STEPHEN STEINHAUS[1] AND NIGEL BARLOW

How do more creative people differ from those who are less creative? What triggers creativity, under what circumstances does it thrive, and how do people foster high levels of innovation? What value and impact does creativity truly have? To find out, we conducted survey research. This provided us with hard data to assess some of the initial hypotheses behind *Re-Think* and explore creativity further.

The web-based survey included 39 multiple-choice questions and nine open-ended questions. Overall, 400 surveys were distributed. Survey respondents included 114 people aged 17–75, living in ten countries, mainly Europe and the USA. The research findings are presented and discussed below.

Given that all of this research is based upon single-source, self-report data, the findings should be investigated in follow-up research. However, many fascinating initial findings and insights did emerge from

---

[1] Stephen Steinhaus is the principal of HR Alignment Consulting Ltd, a Chicago-based talent management consultancy specializing in HR analytics, process development, assessment and coaching.

the data. This strongly supports the profile of the creative re-thinker described in *Re-Think*.

In accordance with the basic tenets of *Re-Think,* the vast majority of respondents (82 per cent) thought that creativity was highly important in day-to-day work and activities (not merely something for creative 'types' in the arts, research and marketing). However, only 29 per cent had received any formal training or coaching on creativity and creative problem solving. Interestingly, 75 per cent of the survey respondents reported a tendency to rely strongly upon intuition when problem solving.

CORRELATIONS BETWEEN CREATIVITY AND KEY TRAITS

First, we investigated the relationship between different personal traits and creativity. A Creativity Index (CI) was developed by summing responses from four[2] of the thirty-nine survey questions. The CI was then correlated with responses to other questions on the survey. Statistically significant findings suggested the relationships between creativity and key traits presented in Table A1.[3]

The magnitude of the correlations strongly suggests that the factors presented in Table A1 distinguish the more creative from the

---

[2] The CI was based upon the following questions: [(Compared to others, I often engage in creative problem solving) + (People I work with say compared to others I come up with creative/fresh solutions) + (People outside work say compared to others I often come up with creative solutions) + (I tend to be considerably more creative when solving problems than others)]. Values summed were: 5 = strongly agree; 4 = agree; 3 = somewhat disagree; 2 = disagree; 1 = strongly disagree.

[3] The correlations obtained from the survey responses suggest each of the relationships in this table. Correlations greater than 3.5 are listed as exceptionally high, 3.0–3.5 are very high and 2.5–3.0 are high. All were statistically significant.

less creative types. These characteristics of a successful re-thinker are explored in *Re-Think* with practical suggestions for maximizing those tendencies. One of the correlations suggests that more creative people feel there is more opportunity to be creative in their occupations. To some extent, this is indicative of the premise that creativity is not fully used in many jobs. So, there appears to be considerable *headroom* for re-thinking in occupations where it has not conventionally been tapped.

Table A1 Relationship between creativity and key traits

The more creative a person is (*as indicated by the CI*), the more likely they are to...	**Correlations**
... encourage others (e.g., co-workers, partners and children) to creatively re-think issues when problem solving	Exceptionally high
... take pride in their ability to generate alternate solutions to problems	
... believe their creative approach significantly enhances solutions in their day-to-day problem solving	
... believe their creative approach impacts their success	
... believe there is a lot of opportunity to be creative in their occupation	
... have a preference for thinking 'Why not?' or 'What if?' rather than 'Yes, but' when they hear an idea that is new to them	Very high
... be very deliberate about setting aside time for thinking and re-thinking issues when problem solving	
... believe they are more successful than the average person in their occupation	
... imagine the worlds of possibilities beyond what they currently believe	
... follow through and act on their big ideas often	
... seek and periodically attain moments of in-depth insight ('eureka' moments) when problem solving	High
... believe there is generally a better way to do things than has been done in the past	
... rely strongly on their intuition when problem solving	

POTENTIAL AND POWER OF CREATIVITY

It is often said that we use a relatively small proportion of our minds in day-to-day activity. The same can be said about the creative side of our minds. Responses to several questions on the survey were very revealing about the potential and power of creativity:

- 99% agreed that people could be significantly more creative in their approach to problem solving;

- 95% agreed that creativity yields successful solutions that would not have been found otherwise;

- 90% agreed that creativity has its place in day-to-day problem solving in fields outside areas such as the arts, research and marketing;

- 89% agreed that creativity significantly enhanced solutions in their day-to-day problem solving;

- 82% agreed that there is generally a better way to do things than what has been done in the past;

- 81% agreed that their creative approach has been a key factor in their success; and

- 73% agreed that there are many 'new things under the sun'.

Overall, the vast majority of respondents agreed that creative energy is a powerful force that drives solutions and success. In addition, there appears to be substantial potential for tapping our creativity considerably more than we do.

THINKING ABOUT CREATIVITY – THE QUALITATIVE SURVEY

The answers to open-ended questions on the survey provided rich qualitative information. This essentially provided us with an opportunity to open up and peer into the minds of survey participants to clarify:

(a) criteria for being a creativity master
(b) noteworthy creative leaps
(c) creativity triggers
(d) energizing creative contexts
(e) creativity kick-starters
(f) pinnacles of creative endeavour
(g) support from others
(h) the ultimate value of creativity

Here is the qualitative data from each open-ended question in the survey.

Criteria for being a creativity master

When you think of creativity, who are the first two people, famous or otherwise, who come to mind?

The clear 'winners' in this section were Albert Einstein and Leonardo da Vinci, who were each mentioned over 15 times. Richard Branson, Steve Jobs, Isaac Newton, Edward de Bono were next, each being mentioned five times. Additionally, five respondents mentioned their mothers, and another five mentioned other family members.

Some of the reasons why 'the most creative people' were mentioned are provided in Table A2. These points are very telling about the criteria people use to identify the most creative people they are aware of. It appears that the more these criteria are present, the more opportunities there are for highly creative solutions to emerge.

Table A2 Traits of creative people identified by survey respondents

<table>
<tr><td colspan="3">Extraordinary: Developed theories in dimensions nobody could have thought of (Einstein). Asked 'what if?' and 'why?' (Einstein)</td></tr>
<tr><td colspan="2">Resourceful: Made rice stretch (mother)</td><td>Vision and guts: Great vision, guts and intuition (Kamprad, founder of Ikea)</td></tr>
<tr><td colspan="2">Going out on a limb: Achieved so much when all could have gone horribly wrong (Woodroffe, founder of YO! Sushi). Did what was sometimes impossible (Gates)</td><td>Provocative: Was thought-provoking, stimulating, dangerous, exciting and challenging (Lennon and Dylan)</td></tr>
<tr><td colspan="3">Perspective: Saw the world the way no one else did and explained it to others (Einstein). Saw art from a different perspective (Picasso). Saw and illustrated the absurdity of otherwise ignorable solutions (Gallagher, comedian)</td></tr>
<tr><td>Expression: Conveyed emotion through abstract concept (Kandinsky)</td><td>Entertaining: Turned the practical into fun (Philippe Starck)</td><td>Radical: Changed the world with his theories (Einstein)</td></tr>
<tr><td colspan="2">Simplicity: Entertaining and single-minded in terms of communicating (Volkswagen ad). Took simplistic and good ideas (de Bono)</td><td>Perseverance: Articulated the absurd and challenged preconceived thinking (Heath Robinson). Refused to let go of ideas even against opposition (Einstein). Kept his belief and persevered (Dyson)</td></tr>
<tr><td colspan="3">Commercial: Has a different philosophy towards business and ideas (Jobs). Understands what people want and gives it to them (Madonna)</td></tr>
<tr><td colspan="2">Imagination: Created an alternate world from nothing (Disney)</td><td>Visionary: Was centuries ahead of his time (da Vinci)</td></tr>
<tr><td colspan="2">Out-of-the-box: Started from scratch and saw all opportunities (Kamprad). Thought of out-of-the-box, un-orthodox solutions and was unique and visionary (numerous)</td><td>Rigour: Applied rigour to finding new ideas and solutions (Einstein and Michelangelo)</td></tr>
</table>

In some cases, the criteria mentioned apply only to a few of the creative thinkers mentioned (e.g., entertaining, commercial, etc.). However, in most cases the criteria mentioned for one of the great creators are also common to others. Common characteristics among these great creators include a dramatically different way of looking at the world, seeing out-of-the-box alternatives, developing a unique vision for the future, challenging the status quo, and going out on a limb to try something that was previously thought impossible.

The research supports the idea behind *Re-Think* that we all have the capacity to be creative. This is reflected by many people identifying colleagues or relatives in their list of most creative people. We particularly like the response, 'My mother and Bill Gates', and were touched by this one: 'My mother first. We had a big family with little income and she managed to feed, clothe, and mentor us all. In her words, she could always "make rice stretch".' There's a re-think!

Noteworthy creative leaps

> *What's the most striking example you can think of – personal or famous – of someone making a creative leap through intuition?*

A diverse group of creative endeavours emerged, from DNA to Velcro! PC computing (including iPod and the Internet) and Columbus' discovery of a round earth each came up numerous times. Other key examples cited included the discoveries of: (1) the wheel, (2) the DNA model, (3) splitting the atom, (4) theory of relativity, (5) space travel, (6) piston rings, (7) video recording algorithms, (8) Walkman, (9) Post-its, (10) Velcro, (11) Google, (12) e-Bay, (13) stomach bacteria causing ulcers, (14) wealth creation, and (15) alternatives to traditional airlines. This list clearly shows that creativity and re-think have places in all aspects of our lives and endeavours.

One respondent said, 'Columbus knew that he would find something beyond the horizon, contrary to all "knowledge" at the time.' It is this confidence of something beyond the horizon that can motivate many of us towards incredible discovery beyond our everyday perspective.

Creativity triggers

> *What factors have you found to be most effective in triggering your creativity?*

It is often said that 'necessity is the mother of invention.' Some of the survey respondents wrote that this was, indeed, what was behind creativity. Table A3 provides the variety of creativity triggers mentioned and the general themes that emerged.

Table A3 Creativity triggers

Necessity: Failure of existing solutions	**Pressure:** Stress, urgency, chaos
Dealing with the unknown: Having to do something completely different without knowing the pathway, situation without an obvious solution, asking 'What if?' and thinking beyond what has worked before	
Blue Sky: No rules, being allowed to come up with the most stupid idea and then to run with it	**Teamwork:** Encouragement, rapid brainstorming, borrowing ideas, like-minded individuals
Intuition: Childlike approach, not caring what others think, simplification, curiosity	**Tension:** Fighting with people
New experience: Multiple experiences, openness, exposure to new cultures	**Passion and vision:** Stimulating problems, passion about subject matter, feeling that there must be a better way, helping others
Perspective: Seeing things from other sides, upside-down thinking	**Targets:** Challenging targets, lack of targets
Quiet Time: Meditation, peace, first impression, beautiful environment	**Humour and attitude:** Fun, laughing, being silly about possibilities
Input from others: Reading, conferences, interviewing, writing, presentations, research	**Drive:** Being in the zone, desire to succeed

As we found in other areas, Table A3 shows that we all have different triggers, some of which are contrary. For instance, some people prefer a quiet and peaceful space, while others prefer pressure and chaos. Some need tension, while others prefer a more harmonious and supportive teamwork. Some take a blue-sky approach, while others prefer structure. Many creativity triggers are common across most, if not all, people (e.g., necessity, new experiences, input from others). The important thing here is that each person identifies and optimizes the triggers they find most relevant and motivating.

Energizing creative contexts

Where are you when you get your best ideas?

There is a widely accepted notion that creativity requires the context of the *three 'B's* – the bus, the bed and the bathroom. Einstein awoke from his sleep to discover the theory of relativity. Archimedes recognized the theory of displacement while taking a bath – and ran through the streets yelling 'Eureka, I've got it.' Similarly, many of our survey respondents said that they got their best ideas:

- *In the bus.* Car, plane, travelling, walking home in a tree-lined street on a cool night with no traffic.
- *In the bed.* Drifting to sleep, sleeping, trying to fall back asleep at 3:00 a.m.
- *In the bath.* Shower, washing, bathing.
- *In the kitchen.* Peeling potatoes, cooking, washing dishes, early in the morning with a cup of coffee.

- *Through recreation.* In the gym, gardening, horseback riding, walking, jogging, mowing the grass, cycling, camping.

- *Through other relaxing activities.* Drinking wine, reading, playing solitaire, watching TV, on holiday, at the pub.

- *During mentally engaging events.* At meetings, seminars, workshops, hearing other creative types, in discussions with others, building on others ideas, with an engaging colleague.

A few of our respondents said 'at my desk'. However, the vast majority said 'anywhere but at work', with many specifying *not* 'at my desk' or 'in the office'. Having some distance from the problem being mulled over seems to help and is captured by the response: 'Anywhere, but not trying to generate ideas.' It is intriguing that there is an unexpected value in boredom, as observed by the professional who said she gets many of her good ideas 'in boring internal meetings'.

Creativity kick-starters

What are the three most important things you do when you solve problems creatively?

Our respondents offered a variety of different approaches they use to generate creative approaches and solutions. This shows that people are often quite deliberate about ways of releasing their creativity. How they achieve this is summarized in Table A4.

In many cases, what enables creativity is the knowledge of how to unlock the door and kick-start creativity into action. People who are not typically creative often simply do not know how to get the process started. As the table below indicates, there are numerous ways to get creativity flowing. Once it starts to flow, as evidenced in many groups we work with, it can be almost impossible to turn off – stopping it can be like trying to cap an erupting volcano.

Table A4 Creativity kick-starters

Research: Determine information needed, design methodology, look at best practices	**Analyse:** Find the real cause and deep roots, define the essence, evaluate pros and cons, don't make judgements, look for synergies
Find Time: Calendar time, free up time for mundane activity	**Stay positive**: Think positive, 'no' is forbidden, get energized, laugh, have fun
Outcome focused: Visualize the outcome, go beyond short-term fixes, imagine what success looks like	
Incubate: Take time out, relax, focus the mind, think, write, draw, envision, sleep on it, keep turning it over in mind, put mind in free-flow	**Imagine:** Dream, know that there is the right solution waiting to be discovered, stay open, imagine the best solution, look at the edges and why it works sometimes, ask what ifs
Pressure: See the issue as a problem, get worried about the problem, think quick, panic for a while, work under pressure	**Alternatives**: Challenge assumptions, map out options, seek a range of answers, focus on one or two pieces of information, evaluate upside and downside
Involve others: Brainstorm, share ideas, listen, speak to someone you trust, 'get someone to challenge and tear my idea to shreds so I can rebuild it', use a winning team	

Pinnacles of creativity

What is your favourite example of someone re-thinking their life or a problem and successfully pursuing their solutions?

The common themes for major re-thinks that emerged were: (1) responding to tough times, (2) intense focus, (3) challenging the status quo, (4) incredible courage, and (5) dramatic reinvention. Famous examples included Nelson Mandela, Bishop Desmond Tutu, Gorbachev, Gandhi, Apollo 13 engineers, George Soros, Miles Davis, Charles Handy, Leonardo da Vinci, Gauguin, Cokie Roberts, Bill Gates, Steve Jobs, Colonel Sanders, and Ray Kroc (who founded McDonald's at age 55).

As with responses to earlier questions, there were many examples of family members, colleagues and other associates. Examples of major life transitions included: an army officer who became a carpenter, a teacher who became a ticket collector, an IT manager who started a cleaning business, someone who left business to be a gardener, and a prostitute who became a career coach!

One person said that major re-thinkers are people who challenge previous thinking. Another commented, 'the guy who turned Toyota upside down thought differently and had the strength of character to battle the entrenched resistance to change.' Someone else said big re-thinkers include 'anyone who has experienced grief and learned to live their life in a different way and used their grief to enhance their life.' The person who mentioned Gorbachev referenced his personal courage, willingness to re-think and take on huge risks.

A need to change, the courage to overcome resistance, the openness to seek alternatives, and the vision to see a completely new way have led many to the pinnacles of creativity. While these are the features of extraordinary men and women, their attitude and behaviour can be adopted by many to re-think the world around them and the degree to which they use their latent creativity.

Support for others in creativity

> *Think of a time when another person has helped you re-think an important issue. Indicate what led up to the situation, what prompted their support and how things worked out.*

Spouses and bosses were mentioned most frequently. Also noted were grandparents, parents, peers, coaches, mentors and business partners. Types of support included bolstering confidence and self-belief, instilling a drive to succeed, encouragement to face reality, emotional support, providing different perspectives and reframing, providing advice and guidance, challenging assumptions, inspiring and mapping out alternatives. *The most common support mentioned was the role others had in listening and asking the right questions.*

While the most creative people by nature do a lot of internal work to come up with innovations, we are not in this world alone and most creators obtain substantial support from those around them. If we had the opportunity to add people like Bill Gates, Albert Einstein and Leonardo da Vinci to our survey, probably we would have found that other people influenced and supported them in their creative endeavours. It appears to be of great value for creators to reach out and obtain the support they need.

The value of creativity

What would it mean for you to be more creative?

The last question on the survey had to do with the real value of creativity in people's everyday lives. Respondents were very positive about what it would mean to be more creative. Responses included being more successful in life and business, having more fun, improved quality of life, gaining more time, better appreciation for the arts, following up more big ideas, greater fulfilment, new friends, new hobbies, improved business performance, more risk taking, increasing life potential, enhanced self-confidence, more energy, more courage and greater connections with children and family.

These responses are exactly what this book and the practice of re-thinking are intended to achieve. Unlocking the doors of creativity and re-thinking the world around us can only accelerate our accomplishments, fulfilment and ultimate quality of life.

The *Re-Think* team is doing on-going research – and pro-search – about what enables us to become more creative re-thinkers. For further information about this, and if you would like to be included in future surveys (people usually find just doing the survey extremely stimulating), then email nigel@nigelbarlow.com or look at our website nigelbarlow.com.

Appendix 2
Re-think resources

BOOKS

The Deeper Meaning Of Liff, Douglas Adams, John Lloyd, Bert Kitchen (illustrator), Pan, 1992, ISBN 0330322206.

Staying Alive: Real Poems For Unreal Times, Neil Astley (ed.), Bloodaxe Books, 2002, ISBN 1852245883.

Tragically I Was An Only Twin: The Complete Peter Cook, Peter Cook, William Cook (ed.), St Martin's Press, 2003, ISBN 031231891X.

Re-Imagine! Tom Peters, Dorling Kindersley, 2004, ISBN 1405305819.

Bollocks To Alton Towers: Uncommonly British Days Out, Jason Hazeley, Robin Halstead, Joel Morris, Alex Morris, Michael Joseph Ltd, 2005, ISBN 071814791X.

Batteries Included! – Creating Legendary Customer Service, Nigel Barlow, Random House, 2001, ISBN 0712680683.

Yes Man, Danny Wallace, Ebury Press, 2005, ISBN 0091896738.

The Power Of Mindful Learning, Ellen J Langer, OpenGL Architecture Review Board, Da Capo Press, 1997, ISBN 0201488396.

Brainwashing: The Science Of Thought Control, Kathleen Taylor, Oxford University Press, 2004, ISBN 0192804960.

Change The World For A Fiver, A project of Community Links, Short Books Ltd, 2000, ISBN 1904095988.

Blink: The Power Of Thinking Without Thinking, Malcolm Gladwell, Allen Lane, 2005, ISBN 0713997273.

The Lazy Way To Success, Fred Gratzon, Soma Press, 2003, ISBN 0972046402.

The Heart Aroused: Poetry And The Preservation Of The Soul At Work, David Whyte, Spiro Press, 2005, ISBN 1844390098.

Music Of The Mind, Darryl Reanney, Souvenir Press, 1994, ISBN 0285632884.

Descartes' Error: Emotion, Reason, And The Human Brain, Antonio R Damasio, Quill, 2000, ISBN 0380726475.

Mind Maps At Work: How To Be The Best At Work And Still Have Time To Play, Tony Buzan, HarperCollins, 2004, ISBN 000715500X.

Adaption-Innovation In The Context Of Diversity And Change, M J Kirton DSC, www.kaicentre.com.

CONTACTS

For style analysis – adaption-innovation – contact either Dr Michael Kirton, +44 (0)1638 662704, or Nigel Barlow, +44 (0)1865 512301.

For Transcendental Mediation (TM) technique, good European contacts are:

Ireland: Dublin Centre: 00353 12845742;
info@ayurveda.i.e.

Holland: Amsterdam Centre: 0031 20 6326305;
mvu-amsterdam@hetnet.nl.

WEBSITES

These change so often that it's best if you email me and we will provide an up-to-date list. And we'd also like to hear about your own favourite re-think sites. With this caveat, here are a few to start you off.

Creativitypool.com
Whatthebleepdoweknow.com (very thought-provoking film as well)
Worthwhilemag.com
Creativearchive.bbc.co.uk
bfi.org – website for the Buckminster Fuller Institute
Wikipedia.org

About Nigel Barlow

Nigel Barlow is a re-thinker, someone who:

1 helps you think of fresh, different and better ways of running your life, business, or even country;
2 combines philosophy (ideas) with plumbing (practical actions) to achieve this;
3 believes that there's nothing too big or too small to apply re-thinking to; and
4 is an *agent provocateur,* creative speaker and coach.

Contact him at:

The Rethink Project
107 Plater Drive
Oxford
Oxon OX2 6QU
England

Tel. +44 (0)1865 512301/302
Fax. +44 (0)1865 512303
Email: nigel@nigelbarlow.com
Website: nigelbarlow.com

Index

acting as if 256–7
active couch potato 102–3
active learning 104
Adams, James 47
Adaption-Innovation (A-I) Theory
  see Kirton's A-I (KAI) theory
Andreeson, Marc 162
Aniston, Jennifer 40
Apple Computer 5
Archimedes 73
Armstrong, Neil 152–3
assumptions 46–8
Atkinson, Ron 153
Attenborough, David 39
Authentic Happiness 119

Bailey, Bill 157
Bailey Bridge 141
Barrie, J M 245
Bauby, Jean-Dominique 32–3
beauty 171
  absence of 171–3
  beautiful solutions 180–83
  beautiful and useful 175–6
  choice 184
  comparisons 176
  inner and outer 183–5
  natural 1779
  solitude 183
  surround yourself with beauty 183–6
  you are what you see 173–5
Becker, Walter 135
Being There (film) 190
belief iceberg 35–6
beliefs 33–8, 134
Bell, Andy 110
Bettelheim, Bruno 173, 187
Blake, William 172, 176, 214
blue thinking 144–8
  guidelines 147
Bly, Robert 241–2
Body Shop 6
Bohm, David 249
books 61–2, 68–9
Boteach, Rabbi Shmuel 31
both/and thinking 5, 82
brainstorm 85
brainwashing 18
Brooks, Roy 155

Brown, Gordon 93
Brown, Mark 144
Buzan, Tony 86, 104

Campbell, Joseph 191
Chatwin, Bruce 114
Chowdry, Paul 157
Churchill, Winston 95
Citta Slow 117–18
co-creation 131–2
  blue thinking 144–8
  clear goals 135
  common language 135
  innovation 140–41
  innovator/adaptor difference 143
  mutual appreciation 135
  shared beliefs 134
  style 136–40, 148–50
  successful 133–5
  teams and KAI 141–2
  trust 132–3
Coleridge, Samuel Taylor 93
comedians 157–9
communication 149
consciousness 13–14, 20–21, 41–2, 252–3
continuity 10
Cook, Peter 159
Copernicus, Nicolaus 5
creative conversation 33–5
creative distraction 100
creativity 3, 7, 91, 96, 153, 161
  criteria for being creativity master 261–3
  effect of Transcendental Meditation 216, 217, 218–22
  energizing contexts 265–6
  intuition 72–3
  kick-starters 266–7
  new people, new ideas 57–60
  noteworthy creative leaps 263–4
  pinnacles of 267–8
  potential and power of 260
  qualitative survey 261–9
  relationship with key traits 258–9
  support for others 268–9
  triggers 264–5
  value of 269
Creativity Index (CI) 258
creators 115
criticism 233
critics 115
curiosity 39–40
  consciousness 41–2
  cultural 28–9
  fostering 48
  naming 65–70
  and the new 44–5
  new people, new ideas 57–62
  Open-Page thinking 53–7
  questioning assumptions 46–8
  re-discovering why 42–4
  science facts 40–41
  thinking why not? and what if? 49–53
  where you live 62–4
  yes but excuse 50–52
  your own story 64–5

Damasio, Antonio 17, 73
De Bono, Edward 172
Dirac, Paul 180
drawing 87
Dylan, Bob 4, 167, 174

Einstein, Albert 42, 71, 72, 73, 75, 83, 180, 247
either/or thinking 115
emotions 119–20
employment 43–4
enthusiasm 23–5
environment 95–7
Estes, Clarissa Pinkola 242
eureka cycle 74–8

faces, remembering 106–11
Fagen, Donald 135
family rituals 120
 friends 124–5
 hellos and goodbyes 120–22
 keeping journals 124
 sharing mealtimes 122–3
 wider view 124–5
fantasies 28–31
feeling 80, 82–3
Feynman, Richard 152
Fibonacci sequence 177–8
Fisher, Denys 96–7
Ford, Henry 201
form and function 175–6
Fosbury, Dick 4
Frost, Robert 7

Gates, Bill 53
genealogy 64–5
Gibran, Kahlil 223
Gillette 68
Gladwell, Malcolm 77
green thinking 144–7
gut feeling 82

Hadid, Zaha 50
Hagelin, John 249
Hamel, Gary 59
Harvey-Jones, Sir John 212
Heineken beer 93–4
heroes and heroines 31–3
Hicks, Bill 157
Hirst, Damien 192
humour 151–2
 Ah-Aha-Haha continuum 151–2, 161–70
 effective surprise 152–3, 161–4
 imagination 160–61, 168–9
 insight 167
 just for the joy of it 169–70
 seeing the familiar in fresh light 155–8, 164–7
 surrealism 158–9, 168
 upside-down perceptions 153–5, 163–4
Hunterwasser, Fritz 178
Huxley, Julian 18

ideas 72
 generating 161–3, 167
 let them develop 199
 quality of 117
 rehearsing 87
IDEO 119
idleness 93–5
I'm Sorry I Haven't a Clue (radio series) 155–6
imagination 160, 168–9
inner meaning 247–53
innovation 48, 118, 140–41, 162–3
intuition 71–2
 accelerating eurekas 84–8
 bath, bed, bus ideas 72
 decision making 73

deeper levels of thinking and feeling 78–83
definition 73
environment 95–7
eureka cycle 74–8
idleness 92–5
minding the gaps 88–92
role in creativity 72–3
two-second 77
Iron John (Bly) 241–2
Isozaki 50
Izzard, Eddie 157

Jobs, Steve 5
Jung, Carl 73, 81
Juxtapose game 168

Kirton, Dr Michael 136
Kirton's A-I (KAI) theory 136–40, 148–50
innovation 140–41
teams 141–3
Knight, Chris 6
knowing 78–83
knowing pyramid 78–9
Koestler, Arthur 79, 151

Lane, John 176, 178
Langer, Ellen 100, 101, 115
Lennon, John 131
Leonardo of Pisa (Fibonacci) 177
Lewis, C S 90
Lexus 35–6
Liebeskind, Daniel 50
location 62–4
London Review of Books 155
love 235–9, 243, 244
Lovelock, Terry 93–4
Lynch, David 217

Maatha, Wangari 188–9
McCartney, Paul 131
Maclaine, Shirley 129
map is not the territory 22
Marks & Spencer 59–60
meals 122–3, 182
meditation *see* Transcendental Meditation (TM)
memory
failing 111–12
long-term 110
names and faces 108–11
three-minute re-thinks 112
mental set 86
mentors 208
metaphor 164–7, 190, 191–2
Milligan, Spike 192
mind mapping 86, 104
Monty Python 158–9
Moorhouse, Adrian 30
Morris, William 175
Mozart, Wolfgang Amadeus 71–2, 74
Myers-Briggs Type Indicator (MBTI) 81

Namath, Joe 221
names 65–70
remembering 106–11
National Rifle Association (NRA) 157
nature 70, 178
Nazrudin, Mullah 113
Negroponte, Nicholas 58
newspapers 58–60
Newton, Isaac 72

Nicholson, Bill 95
Nissan 68
novelty 44–5, 101, 102

open-mindedness 27–8, 37
Open-Page thinking 53–7, 99, 226
  fire yourself 55–7
  teach yourself ignorance 54–5
Opsvik, Peter 49
organizations are people's greatest resource 116–17
Ouyang Hsui 72

paying attention 99–101
  choosing 115
  experiments 101
  family rituals 120–25
  introduce second element 112–14
  more active mind 102–8
  otherwise attracted 100
  quality of 116
  remembering names and faces 108–11
  slowing down 117–18
  space and place 114–18
  taking a bat's view 118–20
  there's no present like time 125–30
  unfocusing 119
Peel, John 45
perception 11
  automatic nature 20
  believing is seeing/seeing is believing 21–2
  blind spot 150
  borrowing perceptions of others 23–8
  changing 15
  conditioning 19–20, 22
  conventional 20
  deciphering 16–17
  first impressions 13
  generational 27–8
  map analogy 22
  new fantasies 28–31
  new heroes for old 31–3
  perceptual grid 14–16
  selective 22, 28–33
  (self-)awareness 17–19
  spontaneous associations 16
  spring-clean beliefs 33–8
  (un)conscious data 13–14, 20–21
  upside-down 153–5, 163–4
  visitor's 25–8
  visual cues 12–13
personality 245
Peters, Tom 68
physics 248
  particle 251–2
  quantum physics 248–52
  split thinking 250
  string theory 248–9
  Uncertainty Principle 250–51
  Unified Field Theory 249, 252
Pilkington 59
Pinker, Thomas 73
planning 84
Poincaré, Henri 74
praise 233
Preece, Sir William 21
problem of experience 17
problem solving 86–8
  analysis, incubation, illumination 77–8

approach it backwards 4
challenge fundamental assumptions 5
changing assumptions about stereotypes 6
clearing the past 4
combining unrelated fields and people 5
creative 74–8
lateral solutions 112–13
paying attention 100
rewriting the rulebook 6
self-limiting boundaries 5
stand back from problem 94–5
Proust, Marcel 62, 158

re-think
assumption behind 6
awareness of own thinking process 7
beautifying the bland 6
interchangeable with creativity 3
meaning of concept 2
pushing beyond the limits 4–5
re-writing the rulebook 5–6
reasons 1–2
research into 7
reversing the obvious 4, 5
selling a story 6
taking a big risk 4
theory and practice 8–9
thinking both/and 5
red thinking 144–7
relationships 225–6
appreciating another 231–3, 243–4
appreciating yourself 228–31, 243
being in time with partner 246
deeper purpose 227–8
embrace difference 240–43, 245–6
feedback 230, 243
giving and receiving 233
have difficult conversation 233–5, 244
love 235–9, 244
praising 233
refreshing 227
say 'yes' 239–40, 245
there's no ideal 227
you are the expert 226–7
ritam 83
Rodgers, Richard 131
Rolling Stone magazine 4
Rose, Steven 73
Rumi (Persian poet) 130

Schneider, Dr Robert 216
Schweitzer, Albert 231
science 249–50
self-appreciation 229–30
self-awareness 17–19
self-belief 208
Seligman, Martin 119
Sellers, Peter 190
Semler, Ricardo 43
Simpson, Joe 300
sleeping/waking gap 89–90
Slow Movement 117–18
Soros, George 82
South African Truth and Reconciliation Commission (TRC) 4
Spirograph 97
Stair, Brigadier 141

Steely Dan 135
stereotypes 6, 14, 80
Stevenson, Robert Louis 93
stories 187–8
  achieving the quest 209
  bringing home the boon 209–10
  deeper purpose 188–90
  finding helpful agents 207–8
  future story 201–3
  living your story 203–10
  meeting obstacles 206–7
  more than metaphor 191–2
  need for 190
  nurturing 198–200
  the quest 203–5
  setting out 205–6
  today's story 200–201
  writing and living 200–10
  writing your own future 192–8
style 136–40, 148–50
  adaptive 137
  fixed 138
  innovative 137
  inventory 148–9
surrealism 158–61, 168

Taylor, Kathleen 184
Tchaikovsky, André 199–200
teaching 105–6
teams 141–3
thesis-antithesis-synthesis 172–3
thinking 80–82
Thomas, Mark 158
time management 125–6
  important but not urgent 126–8
  what the day is for 128–30
Todo, Eiji 36
Tolkien, J R R 67, 90, 188
Transcendental Meditation (TM) 211–13
  compared with other forms of meditation 217–18
  creativity and re-thinking 218–22
  everyday spirituality 222–4
  how it works 213–14
  practical benefits 221–2
  research on 214–17
Trinny and Susannah 229–30
trust 132–3

ugliness 171–3
Utopia/Dystopia 197

values 35, 36
Vashista 249
Vastu 179
Vishvam, Aham 253
visitor role 25–8

Wales, Jimmy 5
walking 90–92
Walking Society 92
Whistler, James 77
Whyte, David 175, 234
Wikipedia 5
Wordsworth, William 222–3
work-life balance 164
Wright, Steven 156, 157
writing vs reading 103–5

'yes, but' 109, 114
YO! Sushi 118

zooming in/out thinking 163